Endorsements

"From the happily ever-after story book wedding, through the valley of the shadow of death, Donna's transparency in sharing her life's journey with us, proves God's faithfulness through it all. This book will surely encourage and inspire all who read it to never give up and know that God has a plan to restore and redeem all which was momentarily lost. A legacy of faith to be remembered"
Teresa Lydon, Cedar Rapids, Iowa

"Reading this book is an encouragement in glorifying God through adversity...over and over again."
Nora Earles, Damascus, Maryland

Treasures in Darkness

More Precious than Silver, More Costly than Gold

by Donna M. Gallagher

EA Books Publishing
Oviedo, Florida

Copyright © Donna Gallagher, 2019

All rights reserved. No part of this book may be reproduced in any form without permission in writing from the author. Reviewers may quote brief passages in reviews.

Amplified Bible (AMP): Scripture taken from the Amplified® Bible, Copyright © 1954, 1958, 1962, 1964, 1965, and 1987 by the Lockman Foundation Used by Permission.

English Standard Version® (ESV®), copyright © 2001 by Crossway, a publishing ministry of Good News Publishers. Used by permission. All rights reserved.

New International Version (NIV) Scripture taken from The Holy Bible, New International Version ®. Copyright©1973, 1978, 1984, 2011 by Biblica, Inc.™. Used by permission of Zondervan.

The Living Bible (TLB) copyright © 1971. Used by permission of Tyndale House Publishers, Inc., Carol Stream, Illinois 60188. All rights reserved.

Name: Gallagher, Donna
Title: Treasures in the Darkness by Donna Gallagher
Identifiers: LCCN: 2019916677
ISBN 9781945976605
Subjects: 1. Religion > Christian Life > Love and Marriage >
2. Religion > Christian Life > Relationships

Published by EA Books Publishing, a division of Living Parables of Central Florida Inc. a 501c3

EABooksPublishing.com

To my loving husband, Rick.

You are, and always have been, my everything!

Table of Contents

Introduction	iv
Chapter 1: The Fairytale	1
Chapter 2: From Trucks to Trust	14
Chapter 3: Storm Clouds Gathering	20
Chapter 4: The Beginning of the End	26
Chapter 5: Fateful January	34
Chapter 6: Unraveled	41
Chapter 7: Leaving It All Behind	50
Chapter 8: Here We Go Again!	57
Chapter 9: Silent Rage	61
Chapter 10: Spring and Summer	65
Chapter 11: Boss Angel	71
Chapter 12: New Beginnings	78
Chapter 13: Memories and Memorials	91
Chapter 14: Tale of Grace	102
Chapter 15: Restoration	110
Chapter 16: All That I Ever Hope to Be	118
About the Author	121

Introduction

"I will give you treasures of darkness and the riches of secret places so that you may know it is I, the Lord God of Israel who calls you by name." (Isaiah 45:3)

"And make the Almighty your gold and your precious silver."(Job 22:25)

Life has a way of taking us by surprise. We've all heard that "stuff" happens. When things happen to us, even when they are not, at all, our fault, we find that we have choices to make. These choices can significantly impact our destiny; for good or bad.

Treasures in Darkness is my story about choices and consequences. It is also a story about faith, hope, redemption, and restoration. It is actually more than a story. It is a legacy.

The lessons, the gifts, the choices reflected in these pages can be summarized simply by saying that what we learned, what we conquered, what we received in the forms of forgiveness, healing, blessings, protection, and salvation go beyond earthly riches.

It is my prayer that, as you read this book, you will find your own treasures in the dark places of your life struggles. I impart to you the faith to surrender your hurts; to lift up your wounded soul, which invades the deepest secret places of your heart, so that you receive and experience the powerful and wonderful healing light of Jesus Christ.

I pray a spirit of wisdom and truth descend upon you, to set you free, as you absorb the manifestation of God's living word—more precious than silver...more costly than gold.

Lastly, I want you to know that God loves you, just as you are this very moment; beyond what you can understand. He desires to call you His own and to bless you.

We've all made choices we regret. We have all suffered consequences because of those choices, but God is greater than our mistakes. Nothing is beyond His mercy; which is new every single morning.

May you find, within these pages, a small reflection of all that our Loving Father has intended for you.

Chapter 1
The Fairytale

"For I know the plans and thoughts I have for you, says the Lord, plans for peace and well-being, not disaster, plans for a future and a hope." (Jeremiah 29:11)

Many little girls want to be a princess who marries her prince charming. Many young men want to run in to rescue his princess, protect her, and provide for her every need, if not her every wish. And what fairy tale doesn't end with both riding off into the sunset, on the white horse, to live happily ever after?

So, there you have it. The beginning, and the ending, of the fairytale formula. But what about the middle of the story? What about the danger, the drama, the evil adversary? What about the human frailties, the mistakes, the circumstances; which are not your fault, nor under your control? How, like the nursery rhyme, "Humpty Dumpty," do you put all the broken and shattered pieces of a life-of two lives-back together again?

You do it only by, and because of, the mercy of God and the amazing grace He gives; even when undeserved. You do it by the power of forgiveness and by obedience to do what is right. You do it by trusting in the faithfulness of the one, true God; whose unfathomable love and unsurpassed power heals, restores, and truly makes all things new. That is not a fairytale. That is the truth of God's promises; found in His word. But for now, we step back into the illusion of the fairytale.

I was that princess. I met my prince charming in high school. I was a sophomore at a small Catholic school, St. Thomas Aquinas, in Jamaica Plain, Massachusetts, where the females outnumbered the males by an easy five to one. When I say small, I mean small. The entire school was about 200 students. The basketball court was a half-court, we had no cafeteria, and we had limited sports and extracurricular options.

There were two tracts: Business and College. I was in Business; Rick was in College.

My very first encounter with him was during a student council meeting. He says I yelled at him for not having enough school spirit. Sounds like that could have been me; especially if I was feeling passionate about something. I don't actually remember that incident. What I do clearly remember is the first time I saw him.

It was the end of my freshman year, and I attended the school play. He was a sophomore, but this was before the student council encounter, a year later. He was playing a part in the play "Legend of Sleepy Hollow." Rick walked out onto the stage, a skinny, somewhat lanky, blond-haired boy, wearing a leather jacket and pulling the reigns of a pretend horse. I don't remember what he said, but I do clearly recall what I thought.

"Who is he and why I haven't I ever seen him around school before?" Play ends. School dismisses for summer. No further thoughts or contact concerning Rick.

Sophomore year comes and goes with slight and unmemorable interaction between Rick and me; save the alleged yelling incident at student council. Enter junior year and a new page of my destiny begins to unfold.

Somewhere along the way, we began running into each other more often. There I was, dressed in my not-so-flattering parochial school uniform, consisting of green plaid skirt that, by regulation, had to hit at or below the knee, white button-down collared blouse, forest green vest and knee socks. Of course, the girls always folded the waist band of their skirt to hit slightly above the knee, when the sister nuns weren't around! And yet, despite that very not-so-appealing outfit, Rick saw fit to notice me!

One Friday, Rick said he would call me over the weekend. To be honest, I had heard that line before and wasn't going to sit around waiting. My cousin, Joe, had invited me to go for a ride with him and his girlfriend. Joe was a big football fan and had played for a few years, for Canton High, until he, unfortunately, had to stop because of a knee injury. We took the drive to Canton High School to see a football game and ended up back at his house. A short while after arriving, my mom called to say this boy, Richard, from school, called looking for me. She told him we were at the football game. Rick drove through three towns trying to scout me down, but he arrived at Canton High after we had left. I was surprised mom had thought it a big enough deal to call and tell me. Somehow, mothers have intuition that can't be explained. She suggested I try to call him back. I had no idea how to do that. It was well before the days of cell phones, and all I knew about him was that his name was Richard Gallagher. I didn't know where he lived or what his father's name was.

Do you know how many Gallaghers were listed in the local Boston phone book in 1968? Well, there were a lot. How was I going to figure out his number? I made an impromptu decision. I would make one try. I would start at the very end of the Gallagher listing with someone named William T. Gallagher. If that wasn't his home, I would give up. I, reluctantly, dialed and asked for Richard.

You can guess the rest of the story. His father was William T. Gallagher. Rick was home, and we connected! Call it fate, but I call it divine providence and God's favor.

Our first, official date was on a Friday, the day after Thanksgiving, in 1968. Rick asked me to go with him to do an errand for one of the nuns at the school. He arrived at my house to find a kitchen full of my Italian relatives, visiting for the holidays. This skinny, Irish boy bravely stepped into a loud, inquisitive clan of skeptical and protective uncles and aunts. He quickly won over my relatives and my parents with his charm.

I began having lunch with a group of classmates that included Rick and Charlie. It all started out innocently, as the school was so small that many of us intersected on multiple levels. The mid-year homecoming dance was just a few weeks away. With so few males in the school, many of the girls were anxious to know if they would be asked to the dance. Charlie asked me to go with him. Charlie was a nice kid, and we had become good friends, but by now, I had begun to get to know Rick, and I was secretly hoping he would take notice and ask me. I didn't want to hurt Charlie's feelings, but I didn't want to make a commitment–just in case Rick came around to his senses.

I decided to be honest with Charlie and tell him I was hoping Rick would ask me to the dance. Being a good friend, Charlie told Rick and Rick took the hint. He started to pay more attention, and we would go for walks, at lunch, along the Jamaica Plain arboretum that flanked the road near our school.

We went to that midwinter, semi-formal dance in my junior year. Later, we went to his senior prom and my senior prom. At one of those proms, Rick wore a white sports coat and a pink carnation, and I wore a pale blue satin gown, with a long, embroidered train flowing behind me. It was as if we stepped out of a song into a fairytale. We dated for five years and got married on May 27, 1973, at Saint Angela's church in Mattapan Square, Massachusetts.

True to the story, it was a fairytale wedding reception at Longwood Towers, near Boston. My bridesmaids wore tiaras. My floor length veil, trimmed with lace, trailed behind me. The venue looked like a castle in a Camelot setting. I threw my bouquet from a balcony; high above the grand ballroom, overlooking my guests.

There are many wonderful things that I remember about my wedding day, but one thing-one feeling-stands out above all else.

After we exchanged vows, were blessed by the priest, and turned to face the congregation to walk back down the aisle, I clearly felt a presence surrounding me; a shift in the atmosphere enveloping us. I had never experienced anything like this feeling of warmth; like a soft blanket of peace flowing from above and sweetly covering me. I don't know how I knew, but, instinctively, I did know that it was God's pleasure and His presence descending upon us. I knew I was doing the right thing by marrying Rick. In the middle of the '70s era, where free love and uninhibited expression flowed, we had kept ourselves for our wedding night. And God was pleased. I felt it. And I knew he had plans for us, and those plans were for good!

We didn't drive off into the sunset on a white horse, but we did peal out in a new, blue Dodge Charger and honeymooned on Cape Cod and Martha's Vineyard. We returned, a week later, and moved into our first home at 81 Willow Street, North Attleboro, Massachusetts.

Both Rick and I had worked part-time jobs, in addition to our full-time jobs, in order to save the $6,000 down payment. Hard work and strong work ethics were part of our upbringing. Neither of our parents had extra finances, so for anything we wanted, we had to earn the money. Rick caddied at a golf club, during high school. I waitressed at a local diner. After graduation, and some college, we both got full time jobs, and we saved as much as we could.

I would turn 21 in July of 1973, but at the time of signing the paperwork for the mortgage, my dad had to co-sign for me, because I was not yet of legal age.

Our new home was a lovely, raised ranch style on a nice piece of land. It had three bedrooms, a large picture window in the living room, and a wood burning stove. The lower level family room and fireplace made for cozy New England winters. Eventually, we fenced in the back yard, planted flowers and gardens, and put in a swimming pool. The adjacent sandpit was a great place for children to explore, ride dirt bikes and for us to snowmobile. I enjoyed sitting on our back deck; gratefully taking it all in.

We knew, from early on, that we wanted to own our home. We had seen our parents struggle, financially, all of their lives; paying rent and having no equity to show for it. Our parents were proud of us, despite Rick's dad having doubts that we would be able to do this on our own. In retrospect, at the time of this writing, in 2019, it is amazing to think we could put down only $6,000 and own a $32,000 home. Believe it or not, that was a lot of money, back then, and the cost of a typical home. We were proud and loved our house. It wasn't a palace, but for this princess, it was the perfect home.

We put the house to good use by having my younger sisters often spending the weekends-- especially after dad's early death; just six months following our marriage. Our three children, Kimberly, Shaun, and Brian, were born at 81 Willow Street.

My close, grade school friends, Debbie and Al, ended up, very coincidentally, living next door to us. Their children, Michelle and Michael, became best friends to our children, Kim and Shaun.

We hosted summer pool parties and rode snowmobiles in the winter in the sand pits next to our yard. We met wonderful neighbors, like Don and Marianne, whose son, Brian, became our son, Brian's, best friend, in younger years.

I had always had a connection with God. Raised Catholic, I learned the catechism, received the sacraments, and prayed. But more than the formality of religion, I often sensed God's love for me. I recall walking home from school and talking to God. On one, particularly brilliant, autumn day, I looked up at the splendor of the leaves overhead and prayed, "Lord, let my prayers and my love for you be as many and as beautiful as all the leaves covering all of these trees."

We started hanging out with my cousin, Joe and his wife, AnnMarie. Rick, Joe, and Joe's younger brother, Paul, were in a band. We would spend time at Joe's parents', my Aunt Audrey and Uncle Joe's home, where the band practiced weekly. Uncle Joe and Audrey were the first in my father's family to become saved, born-again, and Holy Spirit-filled.

After a while, Joe began to cancel band practice. He and AnnMarie explained they were now going to a bible study on Tuesday nights.

They invited us, but we didn't want to go, at first.

Rick was away at his annual National Guard week, doing his duty. Joe invited me, once again, to check out the prayer meeting. I agreed. I was completely surprised by how alive it was. I learned a lot about the Bible that I had never been taught. But what was so intriguing to me was that I felt that same warm and loving presence surrounding me that I felt on our wedding day. I knew, instinctively, that the Spirit of God was in that place. I learned that to know *about* God is very different than knowing God through a personal relationship.

When Rick returned from his week away, I tried my best to explain this unique meeting. He trusted my instincts and agreed to go with me the following week. We became regulars at my aunt and uncle's home; learning more about the Bible and experiencing the wonderful presence of the Lord. Through these meetings, we came to have a personal relationship with Jesus Christ; now, our Lord and Savior. That ultimately led to our attending Faith Bible Chapel, a local, non-denominational church, where we learned about the Bible, grew in the knowledge of God, and grew in friendships and community, for us and our children. Again, to know about God is very different than knowing God through a personal relationship with Him.

At Faith Bible Chapel, we met Rick's future business partner, Rob, and his wife, Melanie, who became my best friend. We met Carol and Lee, Betty and Joe, Sal and Josephine, along with many other wonderful friends, who would play an instrumental part in our story. Faith Bible Chapel was our home church. It was where we were water baptized on a chilly day in May—on our anniversary. It was where we dedicated each of our children to the Lord.

Life at 81 Willow Street was good; very good. Yet, we had challenges as we dealt with dad's untimely death, my mom adjusting to becoming a widow at age 43, and my three younger sisters, who had their share of challenges growing up in turbulent times.

Our first Christmas was only two weeks after dad's passing. Mom was numb with grief. My three sisters were young, the youngest only 10. We had to rally and make Christmas happen for them at our home. Mom had not been prepared and we had to scramble to shop, finance, and wrap gifts for these young girls, who were also devastated at the loss of their dad. Being the oldest, I had the most memories and time with dad, but for a long while after, I did not have time to properly grieve, as my focus had to be on my mom, who could barely function, and on providing a sense and place of stability for my kid sisters. Rick and I became surrogate parents to them. This was a role that a very young, inexperienced married couple would have to quickly grow into and sustain for many years, through many stormy seasons.

But, despite all of that, life was still very good. I was happy being a stay-at-home mom. I had great friends. I had family close by. I had my grade school best friend living next door. My husband supported me. Our kids were healthy and happy. I loved New England. I could pack up the kids on a summer day and head in almost any direction to the ocean. Newport Beach, Fall River, Horseneck Beach, Cape Cod–even the white mountains of New Hampshire–all a short drive away.

I always said, "New England is so beautiful that I feel God bends down lower to touch the sky there; to sprinkle the flowers with joy and to paint the autumn leaves so vibrantly ablaze with orange, red and gold. Then, He blankets the ground with cold, but cleansing, pure, white snow in grand gestures that let us know He loves us."

Never, in my wildest dreams or imagination, did I want, or think, I would ever have to move away from it all and start life over. But, sometimes, life has a way of taking charge.

Or is it God that takes charge and rewrites the fairytale?

Chapter 2
From Trucks to Trust

"Trust in the Lord with all your heart; do not rely on your own understanding and He will direct your steps."(Proverbs 3: 5-6)

From the first time I met Rick, he worked for his family company, Heidke Trucking and Warehousing. He worked part-time, while in high school. Often, we could not leave for a date, on a Friday night, until after 8:00 p.m., because he worked late in the warehouse. Starting from the bottom, he learned the trucking and distribution business and moved from warehouse grunt to traffic manager. Heidke was started by Rick's grandfather, on his mom's side, and, ultimately, owned and managed by his four uncles, for whom he worked.

One evening, a horrible roadside accident took the life of his uncle Ralph. His uncle was chaining two tractor trucks together, in order to tow one of the disabled trucks. As he stood in the middle of the two trucks, another vehicle hit the one that was in the back, pushing the two together; crushing and killing Ralph. Though the accident was a great tragedy, God used it for good; resulting in all of Ralph's children giving their lives to Jesus. It changed their family in many ways but surrendering to Jesus, knowing that no one is promised tomorrow, gave comfort in the midst of pain. Soon after, the remaining three uncles sold the business.

Rick was kept on by the new management, and the company was now called Heidke-O'Donnell. He worked there for a few years, until a colleague offered him a management position at a startup venture. After a short while, I sensed a growing restlessness in Rick. This opportunity had not turned out as promised.

Rick would throw out concerns, from time to time, and daydream about owning his own company one day. To me, it was just chatter. We were young, had a growing family and no extra money to invest in a business. Yet, conversations often revolved, loosely, around putting plans in place to make this a reality.

Even so, I did not expect what happened on that fateful afternoon. Rick came storming in after work, threw his car keys on the kitchen table and informed me that he had quit his job. No discussion or agreement between us had predicated this unexpected action. But he had reached a breaking point, and it was done.

Some of what gave him the courage to do this was the early stage preparation and talks that he and our dear friend, Rob, had been having about starting Rick's own business. Apparently, the plans were further along than I realized. Steps were now put in place to open Northeast Distribution Company (NORDCO).

Rob was in the financial industry. He would become a silent partner; providing the starting capital. He drew in several investors.

The pieces to start NORDCO began to fall into place. Rick rented an empty warehouse in Randolph, Massachusetts. He worked hard to get all of the office systems, warehouse racking, and employees in place. He leased tractor trailer trucks to deliver products that were to be stored in NORDCO's warehouse.

Rick provided the expertise and drive. Within one year, the empty warehouse was almost full. Rick landed several national accounts and was personally responsible for taking NORDCO from zero to a million dollars in revenue after only one year!

The trucking industry, at that time, was technically, not an open market. Rick remembers being contacted by the owner of another trucking company, located not too far from NORDCO. The story goes that the gentlemen extended an invitation for Rick to come and meet him and see his business. I was not there, but, as Rick tells the story, it was like something out of the Godfather, where this man, with gold chains cascading down his neck, sat across from Rick and asked Rick who his customers were and who he planned to go after for business. The meeting was clearly intended for Rick to be politely, but forcefully, told who NOT to go after and whose territory not to encroach upon, if he expected his business to survive. Rick left knowing exactly what he should and should not attempt to do. Luckily, he never had intended to go after the particular accounts that were "protected" by this gentleman.

I was a stay-at-home mom with three young children and the idea of our paycheck coming from having our own business, initially, scared me. I have always had a need for stability and security. To say I dislike change would be an understatement.

Over time, I saw the business grow, and I admit that I was becoming a bit less skeptical, as life was stable and good. I began to trust that this had not been a bad plan.

We were not financially lavish, but the mortgage was paid, food was on the table, and we were able to enroll Kim into Barrington Christian Academy; a private school
where several of our church friends sent their children.

The boys were growing and enjoyed riding dirt bikes and skateboards. We had good friends, lived in a great neighborhood, attended a wonderful, spirit-filled church, and were very close to family.

Our life was not one of luck, but rather the manifestation of God's favor, blessing, and grace. Living in New England was part of my DNA and this place was more than just a home to me. I was very happy to be able to stay home with my children. I had no aspirations to pursue a career or to be anything more than a good wife and mother, and some day,–when I had time-to be a writer.

Rick was proud of all that he had accomplished. For him, it was particularly important that his dad saw how successful Rick's venture actually was. Rick did not grow up with much, if any encouragement from his dad. His mom was very different; always believing in him and teaching him many things from practical jobs like plumbing to spiritual lessons and how to properly treat a lady. But Rick needed to prove to himself, and his dad, that he could-that he would do this, and do it successfully.

I was proud of all Rick accomplished, despite my initial fears. Each of us had a need, for different reasons, to see this venture through. For me, it was stability. For Rick, it was self-worth. And, for a while, all was well–until it was not.

Chapter 3
Storm Clouds Gathering

"A man lacking judgement gives a pledge and becomes guarantor (for the debt) of another in the presence of his neighbor." (Proverbs 17:18)

Thing were not easy, as we found ourselves in the throes of a startup business. Rick knew logistics, of that I was confident. Rob continued to be mostly a silent partner. We were young and inexperienced. Passion was not lacking, but running a business takes insight, skill, and much more.

It was wonderful to watch as Rick grew the business as well as he grew in confidence. He had loyal staff; consisting of truck drivers, warehouse workers, and a secretary. Clients stored various merchandise–from food products, to shoes, to cosmetics, and other items in his warehouse. It was fun to walk through the warehouse and see boxes piled high on pallets. NORDCO was now a real business and Rick's dream come true.

As with most startup companies, you need cash to operate and to expand. Tractor trailer trucks cost money to lease. Employees expect a paycheck. Utilities need to be paid.

Though the company was making ends meet, in order to expand and improve, the decision was made to take out a business loan of about $400,000. Of course, the bank doesn't give out $400,000 without some collateral.

Rick sat me down and explained that we were going to take out a loan and that we, along with Rob and some other investors, would put our homes up as collateral against the bank note. This scared me to death. I did not know much about business, but I knew such a commitment could have some serious consequences. I recall, very plainly, the conversation we had, as we sat on our waterbed in the master bedroom of 81 Willow Street. I shifted, several times, causing the bed beneath us to gently swoosh.

"But putting our home up for collateral seems like a big risk," I protested.

"It'll be fine," Rick stated. "Rob has run all the numbers, and the bank requires collateral against the loan. Rob is putting up his house. An employee has agreed to put his home up and even one of Rob's clients, a well-known doctor at a prestigious Boston hospital, has bought in with an investment in the business. Do you think Rob would allow this if it weren't safe? It's all part of normal business procedure," he assured me, once again.

I knew, in my heart that neither Rick nor Rob would ever make a deliberate decision that would hurt our families. They were moving in faith and confidence that what we were about to do was a good thing. Yet, I shifted again. What did I know? I was a stay-at-home mom, in my early thirties, with no business background, no college degree, and no real understanding of how these things worked; except for the uncomfortable feeling in my gut! And I was a Christian wife. Wasn't it my job to be submissive and trust my husband? After all, hadn't Rick already proven himself with the way he built up the business? Where did discernment have a part to play in this decision?

Plans moved forward to take out a large loan, with each of the investors putting up significant collateral.

It was an early Spring day. Rick and I headed into Boston to meet Rob. From the very first moment I opened my eyes that day, I felt uneasy. We'd had the conversation numerous times, and Rick continued to assure me all would be OK.

We arrived at the building in downtown Boston, where we were to sign papers for the loan and give the bank our home, as security. The details are laser-etched into my mind.

Entering the massive marble lobby, we stepped into an elevator that rose to the very top floor of the high-rise building. We were escorted, by a receptionist into a large conference room, dressed in mahogany furnishings. We sat on heavy, high-back chairs, at a long oval table with an overlay of polished glass. A credenza, precisely arranged with crystal glasses and a water pitcher, graced one wall, and a bookcase, with brass fixtures and old looking books, rested against a far wall.

A wall of windows stretched across the front of the room, framing a panoramic view of Boston's impressive skyline. But it wasn't the skyline I noticed. It was the thick, grey, ominous clouds that swirled before my eyes. The clouds hung low across the horizontal span of sky before us. They seem to be saying, or rather shouting, "Warning. Warning. Storm ahead. Take cover!"

But all was set in motion. The bankers and lawyers arrived. Rob and Rick were strategically seated next to each other, and I sat quietly next to Rick, trying to process the feeling of impending danger.

Pen was put to paper after paper. It took about an hour to sign our lives away. That hour felt like forever to me. Each time I signed on the highlighted line, legally giving over authority of possession of my home and committing to large, financial accountability, that same feeling in the pit of my stomach churned.

It was done, and our home of 13 years was now a guarantee; the home for which we both worked two jobs in order to save a down payment of $6,000; the home we bought and moved into upon returning from our honeymoon; the home where each of our three children were born and raised; the home that held the best memories of my life. Simple business transaction. Pen to paper. Ink to ink. Or was it ink to blood? Didn't matter that we didn't know what we didn't know. It was legal. It was done!

When all the papers were signed, the principals shook hands, engaged in small talk, and suspect smiles were exchanged. We parted, having received approval for a business loan in excess of 400K, which, for two young, thirty-something kids, was a huge deal in 1984.

The elevator descended down the several floors to the massive marble lobby. We exited onto the street. The dark swirling clouds above our heads seem to swirl faster and faster. A light mist began to fall and soon gave way to a heavy and consistent rain.

It was all so appropriate, so prophetic, so symbolic of what was to come. We just didn't know how or when the storm would erupt!

Chapter 4
The Beginning of the End

"And the angel of the lord encamps around those who fear Him, and (He) delivers them."(Psalm 34:7 ESV)

I honestly don't recall how long after that fateful signing that things began to unravel. Some of my notes say about six months. Suddenly, a problem with the structure of the warehouse became apparent, leaving gaps in the foundation. Some of the merchandise was food product, and other items, that could be affected by weather and the sudden appearance of rodents, due to the foundation gaps.

A surprise inspection, before the problem could be addressed, led to losing one of NORDCO's largest clients. Other clients left, and soon, cash flow became a very big problem. The bank note which we, Rob, and other investors had signed, with the intent of helping free cash flow, was now an albatross around all of our necks. NORDCO was unable to pay its monthly commitment to the bank. The process of foreclosure against each of the signors began.

The next months are a blur in my mind. The storm clouds that had begun to gather on that day in May were now madly swirling with the fury of an impending blizzard. As life raged around us, there are rare moments of clarity, in my memory, surrounding those days.

Most of what I do remember simply crashes and collides together in a long winter fog; thick with fear of the impending unknown. I do remember Rick and Rob working many late nights to try to figure out a way to save the business. I remember many days when Rick would wait and pray that a check would arrive in NORDCO's mail so that he could keep the lights on or the telephones running.

I definitely remember him telling me, on several occasions, not to cash our paycheck until he knew the money had arrived to cover it. Sometimes, that money did not come, and I could not shop for food. Since things were very, very tight, I had to become creative and thrifty. Some days the kids could have only one cookie. Some days no cookies. Pizza became canned tomato sauce on toast without the cheese. I tried to fake a nonchalant attitude that this was very normal. All kids had English muffin or toast pizza with no cheese!

December and the holiday season arrived. I struggled to figure out how to make things appear normal for three young children. After all, Santa was not supposed to be short of cash. We put up the artificial tree; thankfully, we did not have to spend money to buy a fresh one. Melanie and I scoured the paper for coupons (note: the internet and coupon sites did not exist at that time). We shared what we found, bought two-for-one deals, and made gifts, when possible.

I bundled up the kids, one day, and searched a nearby pine forest to collect pine cones. I gathered a large bag, full of skinny long cones, and took them home. I baked the bugs out of them, soaked them so they shrank, and then fit the skinny cones into the holes of a chicken wire frame, formed into a cylinder shape to make a pine cone tree. I strung a small row of lights. Each year, I still light that tabletop tree as a reminder of light in a dark, dark season. Surprisingly, that tree has lasted over 30 years.

To each of my children's family, I have since made and given a pine cone tree. Now, they will learn the meaning behind the gathering and making of that special tree. I pray they see it as a symbolic message that we can always find light in darkness, if we trust and try.

In some ways, the holidays provided a small break from the worries and concerns that heavily weighed on us. We distracted ourselves from thinking of what the future may or may not hold. However, the holidays ended, and the temporary reprieve gave way to reality.

As I cleared away the Christmas decorations, I moved a book on a wooden ledge to find a swarm of insects flying out from the pages. Now, on top of everything, we had a termite infestation in our bedroom! It seemed a bit metaphoric for our life.

As Rick worked longer and longer hours, I spent seemingly endless days and cold nights at home alone with the kids. As I lay in bed late one night, waiting for Rick to get home, I heard scratching behind the panels of our bedroom wall. The scurrying and scratching mice were yet another thing to deal with. I couldn't sleep with the continual sound; akin to nails across chalkboard. I soothed my raw nerves by crying myself to sleep.

The stress took its toll on me physically. Not one to typically get sick, I ended up with the worst case of strep throat I had ever had. I was so sick, friends had to help care for the children for several days. Rick came home as soon as he was able to care for me, but on many days the burden of trying to salvage the business mandated long hours.

And then, the last straw. The only pet I had ever really liked and cared about, our fluffy white and black Angora cat, Muffin, became sick and needed to be put down. I held her in my arms and stroked her gently for the last time. It seemed one thing too many, on top of all that was happening. But God's timing was perfect. He knew what was about to happen. He knew having a pet would only complicate what was about to become an extremely difficult transition.

The stark reality of this dark season, both in the cold, snowy winters of New England and the fearful uncertainty of what was to come, fell quickly upon us. NORDCO was bleeding money and a decision had to be made.

Rick and Rob agreed that if the company did not turn around and come out of the red by the end of January, they would close the doors and let the chips fall where they may.

Each business day was critical to success or failure. Some employees were let go to reduce costs. One day, a driver started to pull out of NORDCO's truck yard. As he approached the road, the driver touched the brakes to prepare to turn onto the main street. The truck did not stop. Fortunately, because he had not yet built up speed, he was able to maneuver back into the parking lot and stop. Someone had sabotaged one of the tractor trailers and cut the brake lines. If it weren't for the skillfulness of the driver, he, and possibly others, may have been injured or killed. On another occasion a second set of brake lines were cut. We never knew for sure who cut those lines, but we had some theories. I believe angels must have surrounded those drivers. This was just the beginning of things to come against us.

At one point, the bank, which held our loan, was supposed to pay the quarterly taxes.

They did not pay. I assume they were holding onto as much money as possible, to protect their own interests, in the face of an apparently failing business. The IRS did not take kindly to non-payment and they withdrew the money due from our business account, without notice to us. This resulted in the bouncing of some of our employees' final pay checks. We had no way of knowing this would happen and no cash to make it good. We were as angry and crushed as those who were slighted. Rick and Rob were honest men, but all we could say was that we were sorry. Our hands were tied with frozen accounts.

Rob took a week off to clear his head and drove with Melanie to Florida to stay with his mother. He was supposed to mail explanatory letters to employees before he left. In the midst of all the trauma and emotion, he put the letters in his car but forgot to mail them. He realized it when they arrived in Florida, so he mailed the notices from a Florida post office. Unfortunately, the Florida postmark was perceived, by one employee, as confirmation that we had taken the money for ourselves and were now enjoying the good life on vacation. Nothing was further from the truth. We were in jeopardy of losing everything and vacation was not a remote option.

There were scandalous rumors that Rick and Rob absconded with money from the company. But perception is reality. Lies can seem stronger than truth. It broke our hearts to know we were thought of this way. We could not convince the employee otherwise, and a rift, the size of a canyon because of a false perception, was forced between Rick and one of his dearest employees—a man who had put his trust in Rick and the business.

Even years later, our hearts ache that this man would not allow us to explain, nor accept what was truth. Such is the work of the enemy; the father of lies, who comes to steal and destroy truth–God's truth–all truth.

Yet, despite it all, we understood this man's pain. For he, too, had much to lose in all of this. I pray the years have caused him to heal and that one day we may see him again.

Things did not end there. Rick began receiving death threats. He kept a billy club in the pocket of the driver's door in his car. And, close by, he also kept a gun; for which he had a permit. I am not really sure why all of this happened, except that some of his former employees did not understand what was going on and thought they were getting an unfair deal by being let go. To be truthful, I do not know how much was actually explained or if it was even necessary for Rick and Rob to disclose the hardships and details of the business. But two things were for sure. The break lines were cut, twice, and the death threats were very real.

So, the clock began ticking on 31 fateful days of January 1986, as our home, our lives, the business, and our future hung in the balance.

Chapter 5
Fateful January

"We are pressed on every side by troubles, but not crushed and broken. We are perplexed because we don't know why things happen as they do, but we don't give up and quit." (2 Corinthians 4:8 TLB)

Despite Rick and Rob's best efforts, January ended with NORDCO still in the red. They would close the doors, as soon as all the loose ends could be tied up. Of course, this was not as simple as it sounds. Our homes were tied to the bank's collateral note. Our emotions were tied into all the effort that had gone into building and sustaining the business. Our future was tied into it all.

I tried to appear as normal as possible for the kids. But often, my thoughts were elsewhere. The uncertainty of the days ahead and the knowledge that it was only a matter of time before the bank took our home, was a constant and miserable companion.

I remember a parent-teacher conference for Shaun. I tried to be present, but my mind was not there. I didn't recall a thing the teacher said. I barely made it through without bursting into tears.

I went food shopping, one day, and put the few meager bags into the shopping cart and wheeled them out to my car. I absent mindedly headed home without putting the bags in the car. Fortunately, when I realized this, I called the store, and someone had brought the cart inside and held it for me.

Another time, I visited my mom for her birthday. I had a small present for her and put the box on the roof of the car, while I helped her into the car and strapped in the kids. I, then, drove off with the present on the roof. It flew off and I never did find it!

I decided I needed something to deal with the stress and help bring in money. I had been attending an aerobic dance class. I liked the way I felt after and enjoyed the style of dance. I researched how I could get certified to teach this class, even though I had never taught.

I boldly went to the local YMCA and convinced the program manager to allow me to teach and use the facility, at no charge. He agreed. Even though, most days, I had no desire to see anyone, but rather wanted to crawl under the covers and escape the world, I made myself lead the class a few times a week. I needed the accountability to get up in the morning. I knew it would be good for me physically, as the stress was higher than I had ever experienced in my life. Though it did not bring in much money, every dollar helped. This experience also taught me that I could do anything I truly set my mind to doing. Little did I know, I would need that lesson in a much bigger way very, very soon.

Rick and Rob worked to tie up loose ends. An auction was scheduled to get rid of any unleased equipment. The money would go to write down the loan. Rob made most of the arrangements for the auction. It was so emotional for Rick, he could not make himself go into NORDCO on the auction day and see all of his work, and his dream, scavenged by bargain hunters.

One big problem remained. Technically, the bank owned three of the four investors' homes; including ours. That was the collateral we put up, in May, when we signed those papers. Now, Rick was out of work and unable to pay back the bank. Foreclosure was looming on the horizon.

Through all of the emotional roller coaster that I had been riding, I selfishly did not pause long enough to reflect upon how devastating this was to Rick. I knew it was difficult, but my selfish eyes did not truly see his pain. He is a quiet person, by nature, and because he did not often verbalize his emotions, it was foolishly easy to assume he was dealing with it all. I didn't know he was overcome with condemning voices that constantly and silently tormented him, in a mocking whisper, saying, "*You have failed. You have failed your business. You have failed your family and yourself."*

How destructive our own thoughts can be. It is no wonder that scripture warns us, "As a man thinks in heart, so he is" (Proverbs 23:7). We are all subject to condemnation, but if we have put our hope and trust in Jesus, then we know we are cleansed, forgiven, and He promises to work all things for our good--even when it seems like life is falling apart.

But how much easier it is to quote verses and talk about faith years later, than in the moment of trial and despair. This became very evident, concerning Rick, as he finally allowed his emotions to let loose.

It wasn't until one night, as Rick lay on the coach staring at the ceiling, sniffles quietly masked, that I saw the depth of his hurt. The winter icicles that hung from outside the picture window, facing the couch, looked like silver daggers against the cold black night sky. The accusations screaming in Rick's head were like daggers to his heart, piercing his self-confidence and striking a near fatal blow to his faith. I sat next to him, finally putting my own selfish feelings aside, for probably the first time in months, and hugged him. His brave face cracked, and the tears rushed down his cheeks, as he broke and fell deeper into my arms.

"I'm sorry," he whispered. "I'm scared and I am so sorry." Silence was the only response I recall. What was done, was done. It wasn't his fault, but he felt the weight of it all crashing upon him. He felt like he had let us down and could not provide for his family. I pulled him closer and we cried together. I was scared too. Scared of losing our home; scared of the unknown; scared of not being able to pay bills. But, together, we would figure it out. We just needed to know what to do next.

It could have been easy... should have been easy, or at least simple. Find a new job, pay off debt, and go on with our lives. But "should have" and "could have" was not the way it played out. We were weak and tired. The January avalanche was rolling faster and faster toward the center of our lives. We were on a collision course with destiny.

God's sovereignty is rarely recognizable in moments of great pain. It takes a greater hand, with a greater plan to steer one through a path of destruction in a way that we avoid being destroyed. The problem is that the hand of sovereignty is often invisible and seen only through eyes of faith.

Sometimes–so many times–in order to create something new, something better, something stronger, the old must be destroyed. A demolition must take place before a new structure can be built. This is a messy process that can leave things appearing to be in total chaos. But, behind the scene is a loving God who carefully takes the brokenness and turns ashes into beauty; if we allow Him.

Everything familiar, everything we thought to be true was about to be challenged. Many things we held near and dear would be ripped from our arms and tested. The familiar was about to be traded for the unknown. Faith would no longer be something we read about or loosely professed. It would become the lifeline we would need to survive. Trust would be the anchor that kept us from drowning in a sea that seemed to be swallowing us up, amidst a series of violent storms.

As I prayed and pored over scriptures, I saw myself shipwrecked in a raging tempest. The pieces of my lifeboat were strewn all around, as huge waves kept crashing around and over me. The only way I could survive was to grab a piece of driftwood and hold on to it with every ounce of strength in my being. God said to me that the driftwood symbolized His Word and His promises. I had to hold my neck and head up high to avoid swallowing the furious waters. Looking up meant I had to keep my eyes on God. Looking forward, into the future, was terrifying, and looking down, into the past, was too painful. The only place to look was up!

"Now when these things occur, look up and lift your head because your redemption is near." (*Luke 21:28*)

I had no choice but to believe, by faith, that He would work out all things for our good (Romans 8:28). I've heard it said that sometimes your breakthrough is in your breakdown. Rick would have to navigate his own walk with God, in his own time, and in his own way.

For me, I read and re-read the scriptures. Praying them. Pleading them. Crying through them. All I heard was silence. Sometimes it seemed like I was going down, for the third time. And all I could do was close my eyes and hold on for dear life.

Chapter 6
Unraveled

"Though You Slay Me, Yet, will I Trust in Him."(Job 13:15 KJV)

Winter began to give way to spring. Spring, in New England, is cool and crisp. First, the crocuses peer through the last layer of snow. Then, the tulips proudly arrive and dance in the warm and welcomed sun. Finally, the lilacs fill the air with sweet perfume, and the grass lays her carpet of green.

Our yard was filled with all of these flowers and more. I loved to plant flowers and waited anxiously each spring to walk around the yard and enjoy the beauty of God's creation. I thought back to many years of digging on my knees, glancing often at the boys riding their big wheels in the driveway or playing in the sandbox. I recall Kim and her friend, Michelle, playing with Cabbage Patch dolls. Sweet memories.

Flowers are a miracle to me. From a seed comes beauty, pleasure and a reflection of the greatness of God. But this spring of 1986, I noticed none of it. Once the loose ends of NORDCO were finalized, Rick's critical task was to find a job. We had little money coming in; only a small unemployment check and some food stamps. We had never received public assistance, and, though we were grateful, it was humbling. We had almost no savings, except for a few hundred dollars. Since we could not afford daycare, I could only work part-time waitressing. I depended on the kindness of friends from church and the neighborhood to watch Brian, who was not yet in school full-time.

Rick had not been out of work in twenty years. He feverishly put together a résumé, answered unemployment ads, and worked with recruiters. There were no online job sites back then. He landed several interviews over the course of a few months, but the strangest things happened time and time again.

The interview would go really well; and then, something out of left field would happen, and he would not get the job. One example was with a company where Rick hit it off famously with the future boss. Rick was more than qualified for the job, but a review of a profile test by the company psychologist insisted that Rick was "too much like the current man he would work for." They wanted someone who was "less like the boss." Amazingly, the psychologist never interviewed or met Rick but decided his fate from a profile test.

Another time, the job was all but promised to him, when suddenly, they changed their mind for unknown reasons. Absurd things like this kept happening over and over again. We both became very discouraged. Little did we know; an invisible hand was at work. Each of the five companies that denied Rick employment, despite great interviews, all went out of business. Clearly, God was guiding us and protecting us; even when it felt like another setback. What we may perceive as moving backwards, might just be God positioning us to move forward. I see it like an athlete who intentionally steps back in order to gain momentum and speed before bursting forth to break a barrier or cross the finish line.

The clock was ticking, and we had many things to sort out. Summer was half over, and the kids would be starting school in about six weeks. The bank was moving forward with the foreclosure process, and soon we would have to leave our home.

Without a job, we couldn't rent. None of our family in Massachusetts had room to take in five additional people. It is easy to understand how successful people, because of one bad stroke of luck, could lose everything and become homeless. We could have been one of those statistics.

All through this ordeal, Rick had been in touch with my uncle, Dan, who lived in Silver Spring, Maryland. Uncle Dan was my father's brother, and I loved him dearly. Since dad had died so young, my uncle was a surrogate dad to me. Not only did he look a lot like my father, I always sensed a genuine care from him. He was a Christian and he was wise.

Dan had been sending Rick employment ads from Maryland, telling us that because they were so close to Washington DC, the region was somewhat recession proof, and employment was more robust than other parts of the country. As the clock moved closer to the time for the bank to physically take our home, Dan and Aunt Stephanie made an offer for us to come to Maryland and live with them, until we could get a foundation back under us. Our hope was, it would only be for a few months, while Rick looked for work.

Dan and Steph had five children, and two were away at college, leaving some empty bedrooms. I had never imagined I would leave my beloved New England, my family, and friends, but it seemed we had no other viable options. The decision was really made for us. By mid-July, plans were put in place. We told our family. With tears in all of our eyes, they comforted and supported us.

Uncle Dan arranged for a storage unit. We made a brief trip at the end of July to register the kids in school and figure out, with Dan and Steph, how all of this would come together. Their household was about to grow from seven to twelve, and a lot of emotional baggage was coming with us. Certainly, this would be an adjustment for them, as well as for us.

One of the most poignant and sweetest memories of this story occurred at this juncture. It will, forever, be etched into my mind. We packed up what we could into our burgundy Chevy station wagon, as we prepped for this July trip to Maryland. The car, filled with items to put into storage, had room left only for the children. We decided to leave at three in the morning to allow the kids to sleep most of the eight-hour trip. When the time came, Rick scooped up each child, in their PJs, and carried them to the car. When he went into our nine-year-old son's room, Shaun lifted his sleepy head, and Rick noticed he had been clutching something as he slept. With eyes half-open, he released his tightly clenched fist to reveal a few quarters that a friend had given him.

"Here, Daddy," he said, "These are for the tolls on the way to Maryland." Tears streamed from my eyes at his tender, giving, and willing heart. It was all he had, but he wanted to help. Shaun still has a tender and caring heart, to this day. I cannot relay this story without tears flowing and touching my soul.

As planned, the children slept much of the way, and we pulled into my uncle's driveway mid-morning. There was much to do in a short time. We registered the kids for school, and both of us needed to look for work. We had to figure out which of our belongings would fit into Uncle Dan's home and what needed to be moved into storage. We checked off as many tasks as we could and gratefully returned home, to Massachusetts, to execute the plan.

The next few weeks were busy and tearful. I carefully packed years of memories in newspaper and paper towels. Many friends came by to help. Melanie did not. It was too painful for her. I ached for her to comfort me through this emotional time, but I understood why she could not.

Months later, I found out that she did come by and help clean the house and sort through some things we left behind. She discovered a note scratched on the closet wall, written by our 11-year-old daughter. It simply read "I love this house." It was Kim's way of saying goodbye. How could a child process this pain, when we, as adults, could barely do so?

We filled our calendars with goodbye dinners with family and friends. Our dear friends, Carol and Lee, threw a going away party, and many of our Faith Bible Chapel friends came to wish us well. I still remember the heart-shaped going away cake. I loved these people and my heart broke as much to say goodbye to them as it did to say goodbye to my mom and three sisters.

On our last Sunday service at Faith Bible Chapel, the pastors called us up, laid hands on our family and prayed. Pastor Sal, a kind and prophetic man, spoke over us that God would protect us and keep bitterness from our hearts. How relevant those specific words would become.

Pastor Sal's prophetic prayer said that though this season of pain may feel like the Lord's rejection, it was a necessary season of pruning. The vinedresser must cut deeply for new shoots to grow in the right direction. Though He wounded, He would heal us. We were admonished to not forsake the Lord, but to trust and watch what He would do; for joy comes after a season of trial. We were told, we were called apart for service, and, not only would we know the way for the misdirected, but we would now have compassion. There were other words spoken and we were given the entire text handwritten and dated August 23, 1986. I keep it in my Bible as a reminder that God fulfilled, and continues to fulfill, His promises and His Word to us.

Finally, the day arrived. The station wagon was packed. I, purposefully, was the last one to walk out the front door. Rick and the kids waited patiently for me in the car as I took my time; memories flooding my mind. I painfully dragged myself through each empty and silent room for the last time. Images flashed before my eyes, as clear and intense as if I were presently there.

Flash! Rick carrying me over the threshold as we returned from our honeymoon and entered this home for the first time as husband and wife. Flash! Each of our children sleeping in their cribs. Flash! The soccer ball and Big Bird birthday cakes. Flash! Rick surprising four-year-old, Kim, with a kitten. Flash! Our first Christmas tree; the same year dad died and the same Christmas, despite a huge snow storm, my aunt Irene and family made their way over treacherous roads to be there with us for Christmas dinner. Flash! Shaun riding his skateboard, wearing his famous black, half-shirt. Flash! Summer pool parties and long winters snuggled by the wood stove.

Finally, I knelt down in the small bedroom with the royal purple rug; tears stinging my eyes and rushing like a river down my cheeks. I mustered what little strength I had left. With words I could barely speak, choking in my throat, I muttered a sincere, but grief-filled prayer, "Lord, I don't understand any of this. We prayed and trusted You. I believed You would save our home, but You did not. Even so, thank You for the years and good times that You have given us here. *Though You slay me, yet will I trust You.* Bless the people that end up living here and may Your Spirit remain here for them as You did for us."

I put my hand on the door knob, took a deep breath, closed it for one final time, and slowly walked down the front steps. I, hesitantly, got into the car and did not look back. Not that I could have seen, if I had looked back, because my eyes were blurred, red, and almost swollen shut. My scarred and broken heart felt as if a heavy brick was pushed onto my chest. I sat; silently unable to speak or even think.

Rick drove as I drifted in and out of sleep, trying desperately to stop the pictures and memories that flooded my mind. Questions haunted me. Why didn't I protest more? Why did God allow this? Will the kids be OK? What about Rick and me? Can we make a new life and new friends? Will we find jobs?

I must have cried myself exhausted most of the way to Maryland. This was not supposed to happen; not to us. We were the picture-perfect couple; the princess and her prince. We had the perfect life. What was going to happen to us now?

Chapter 7
Leaving It All Behind

"But one thing I do, forgetting the things that lie behind, and reaching forward to what lies ahead, I press on toward the goal to win the (heavenly) prize of the upward call of God in Christ Jesus." (Philippians 3:13-14)

Who knew, back in 1980, when Rick and I took a trip to Washington, DC to participate in a Christian rally on the grounds of the historic Washington mall, that the still, small voice that Rick heard that day, saying we would one day live near D.C., was God, speaking truth? Never did I imagine I would leave my beloved New England. Little did I know, then, what was ahead. Yet, in August of 1986, here we were living out the manifestation of that prophetic word.

We arrived in Maryland about 10:00 a.m. on a Thursday morning. We pulled into the long driveway on Magnolia Road with our station wagon and the small U-Haul trailer filled with what we were able to take. I entered Uncle Dan's house emotionally exhausted and with red, swollen eyes.

Stephanie greeted us and gave me a long, tender hug, whispering in my ear, "Welcome to your new home." I can still hear her sincere and loving words. We all shared breakfast on their shaded porch, and then, I retreated to the lower basement, which would be our space, and I cried again, until I, finally, fell asleep.

The transition to Maryland was not easy for any of our family. Each of my children had to adjust to new schools, new friends and new circumstances such as mom working. If only I had the understanding and emotional ability to help each of them navigate this tumultuous time. I did not. I did the best I could, but it has always been a deep regret that my own emotional roller coaster did not allow me to see, or understand, how our upheaval impacted each child differently.

It seemed that each day presented a new challenge to overcome.

Our unemployment and food stamps, from Massachusetts, were no longer applicable in Maryland. Because we had not worked in Maryland, we could not collect; making it more urgent for both of us to find employment.

I had not worked, professionally, in over ten years; choosing to stay at home with the kids. My marketable skills were limited. I prayed, "God let me find something that is close to where my children go to school so I can stay close and still be part of their lives."

I applied for a clerical position at a pool and spa store, just down the road from home and within walking minutes to their elementary school. The job was a cashier and store clerk. I really liked the family who owned the business. They were willing to hire me, and we set a start date.

The morning I was to begin the new job, I excitedly dressed. Aunt Steph would be there to send the kids off to school and to greet them when they returned. She was great; always baking homemade snacks. I remember the smell of gingerbread muffins with chocolate chips. I felt comfortable with them in her care, but sad that I had to exchange my role as full-time mom for part-time mom and employee. As I finished my last sip of coffee, preparing to walk out the door, the phone rang. My boss, Joanne, was on the other line.

"Donna, I am sorry to tell you this on such short notice," she said hesitantly. "But there's been a change and the job is no longer available." I was speechless and caught my breath enough to mutter, "But you offered me the job and I am just about to walk out the door. How can this be?" "I know," she said sheepishly, "but it is complicated. My father has decided he wants to help at the store, and we cannot afford both of you. I am so sorry."

I hung up the phone, in shock, and sat at the small, round kitchen table; attempting to explain to Steph what I really did not understand. We both just stared at each other in disbelief and lingered in silence over unfinished coffee. I finally broke the silence and struggled to ask what seemed the unanswerable question. "Where is the victory? Where is God in this? This job seemed the perfect answer to my specific prayer of working close to home and school." My head was spinning with questions and confusion.

Steph thought for a long moment and responded with what I am sure was a desperate attempt to comfort me. But what she said was divinely inspired and has stayed with me for over 30 years. "Sometimes," she quietly said, "the victory is in just getting through the day." And then, Steph prayed with me. I don't remember what she prayed, but the response was instantaneous.

Suddenly, the phone rang, again, and broke my thoughts. It was Joanne. "The job is still yours, if you want it," she said. I never did find out what happened within their family to create the change of mind, but I am sure God had everything to do with it.

Sometimes the victory is in just getting through the day! These words have sustained me over and over again. I have shared them with my own daughter in her darkest moments. They remind me, consistently, of the need to bring all things to prayer, to fight for what we believe God has promised, and to remember, God can instantly change a circumstance.

My friend, Shelia, often reminds me of the verses in the Bible that start with the word "suddenly." And suddenly, Jesus appeared. As in Bible days, He appeared on that day in my aunt's kitchen. It was a supernatural "suddenly."

It shall also come to pass that before they call, I will answer; and while they are still speaking, I will hear. (Isaiah 65:24)

I started my new job. It was a gentle transition into the working world, and I was grateful. This was truly an answer to specific prayer. The days slowly began to take on a sense of normal. We began to cobble together a new life.

My cousins, Maria, Tina, and Liz, were actually closer to Kim's age than mine, and became like sisters to Kim; especially Tina. The boys found new friends in the neighborhood and in school. They seemed to adjust fairly well. Even so, the traumas of moving and the stress of what we went through seeped into the children in insidious ways.

One child started sleep walking. After a few weeks, Stephanie noticed a foul smell coming from a bedroom. Apparently, during sleep walking, this child was getting up and peeing in the corner of the room; completely unaware of doing so!! This was another neon sign that the disruption of our lives affected the children too. Fortunately, this was short-lived, and I began to try to notice where each of the children needed individual and particular attention.

There were many good memories while we lived at Uncle Dan's. When his boys came home from college, we had a full house. The dinner table was set for 12. There were jokes and sometimes the throwing of dinner rolls across the long table. There were ice cream runs, where Rick and I took the girls for outings. There were walks with Kim and Liz to see the horse farm down the road. There were fresh cookies that Stephanie baked for the kids after school, almost each day. There were many evenings sitting on the big back porch, sipping a glass of wine with Uncle Dan or reading a book or just feeling like we had a home; even though temporary.

There were also challenging moments. Uncle Dan was not used to chatty and active boys greeting him each morning when he wanted to have a quiet cup of coffee or pray. Stephanie had extra meals to plan and cook and extra cleaning, since I was working.

As grateful as I was to be there, there was not a place to go to be fully alone. I cried, often, as I missed home. Nothing on the walls or in the house was mine. I missed my home, my things, my mom and sisters, my friends, and the beach that was now a 2-3-hour, one-way drive over the Bay Bridge. There were nights I would cry myself to sleep and there were nights

I could not sleep. I began taking NyQuil so I could drift off. It became a kind of a family joke, and Stephanie even bought me a large gift-wrapped bottle for a birthday present! In retrospect, it is easy to understand how people turn to alcohol or drugs in desperate times. Fortunately, my Nyquil habit did not last long.

Rick looked desperately for work. Nothing seemed to open up, despite his willingness to take just about anything to support his family. It was, as the author, Charles Dickens, said, "the best of times and the worst of times."

Chapter 8
Here We Go Again!

"With weeping they shall come; they will pray as I bring them back. I will lead them back, I will make them walk by brooks of water, in a straight path in which they shall not stumble, for I am a father to Israel, and Ephraim is my firstborn."(Jeremiah 31:9 NIV)

I liked my job at the Pool store. The family took me in. For about a month, they were able to use Rick part-time to help with pool closings. Through the store, Rick was given a contact name at the local United Parcel Store (UPS) for delivery work through the holiday season.

Rick was willing to take any job offered and do whatever he could to support his family. He worked long hours, delivering packages, mostly, to apartment buildings, which required going up and down lots of stairs. He couldn't come home until all the packages for that day were delivered so he often missed dinner with the family.

There was talk, by his supervisor, that even though his position was temporary for the holidays, he might have a more permanent opening after the first of the year. This was not even close to his dream job, and not what he enjoyed. Yet, he gave the temporary job his best, as he always did; grateful for the paycheck and honoring to God.

It would not be accurate to say that Rick did not have moments of despair and longing for what used-to-be. These feelings came to a head on Christmas Eve, 1986, as he worked late delivering every last package while the family waited for him to be able to come home to celebrate.

About 8:00 p.m., at the end of that long Christmas Eve day, Rick sat exhausted on the stairs outside the building of his last run and cried out to God with tears in his eyes and an ache in his heart. He faced the empty truck and felt just as empty inside. He wanted to be home with his family. He wanted to do the work he used to love. He wanted his better life back. He pondered many dark things in his soul before he finally came home.

We somehow got through that first holiday season. We were grateful for all of the kindnesses shown to us, but we also struggled being away from our Massachusetts family and not able to travel to see them. I missed our unique holiday traditions. I, often, was very sad and lonely.

UPS notified many of their temporary seasonal workers that they were laid off, now that the holiday season was over. Rick was among them, but he was told there was still hope of more permanent work after the first of the year. We waited and waited, but no call ever came. One day, Rick spotted his former supervisor delivering packages. He knew, then, that he was not going to be called back.

Ironically, because the pool season was over and the spa store was very slow, I was also let go with a loose promise of coming back when spring arrived. This was a double blow. Now, we were both out of work and it felt like all the progress of the last four months brought us back to square one! With the dark, cold winter settling in, we, once again, found ourselves fighting despair and desperately trying to hold onto faith.

I began to withdraw; opting to spend time alone in the bedroom of the dark and isolated basement. Depression is like a fog that slowly begins to descend until it finally covers you. It is something one must fight and fight with God's help or it will win.

We searched the employment ads again and again. I answered an ad for a clerical position in a shoe store. Rick answered an ad for a position at a uniform supply store in Washington DC. We both were hired in February of 1987.

We did our best to handle each day, as it came. Steph continued to care for our children. My new job was not as close to the kids' school, so I was less flexible. Somehow, we plugged along and still prayed. Little did we know that, true to His word, God's invisible hand was at work, and we were right where we needed to be, for this season. He had plans that were being orchestrated by His kind, but unseen hand. Our part was to trust in the waiting as He directed our steps. Easy words to pen, but not so easy to live!

Now, as I look back years later and see how the plan evolved, oh how I wish I had just trusted with all my heart. I would have avoided so much anxiety and stress. When God says He knows the beginning from the end, we need to believe Him. We are often living the middle chapters of our story. The last chapter is not yet known, despite what we project onto the future. Faith is the pen and trust is the ink that imprints the pages of our personal book of life. Faith is believing what is not yet seen. Trust means to rest in peace in the midst of the trial. However, these were lessons that I had yet to learn.

Chapter 9
Silent Rage

"Refrain from anger, and forsake wrath! Fret not yourself; it tends only to evil"
(Psalm 37:8 ESV)

When we first moved into Uncle Dan's home in August 1986, Rick and I had hoped it would be for only a few months. Dan and Steph wisely knew it would be for closer to a year.

Things seem to flow into somewhat of a routine. The children were settled in school. Kim had fun sharing a bedroom with Tina and doing sister-like things with Liz and Maria. The boys were learning soccer skills from their older cousin, David, or hanging out with Dan, Jr., when he was home. I can only tell this story from my perspective, but now in retrospect, I know it must have been very difficult for all of them to have our family of five invade their home, their private spaces, their belongings and their time.

Some memories stay with me, even now, over 30 years later. One is my uncle retreating to his bedroom, just to escape the noise and bedlam; especially of my two boys. Another is Steph carefully scouring recipes to find nutritious, but economical, meals to feed 12. I can vividly recall my petite aunt using two hands and all her muscle to pick up the biggest, cast iron frying pan I had ever seen to make something called "Idaho Chowder!" Once the meal was cooked, she would, somehow, muster up all her strength and carry that full and heavy pan from the stove to the dining room table. Fortunately, being an Italian family, there was always good food, and pasta managed to miraculously multiply to feed even our ravenous bunch.

These may seem like silly or insignificant memories, but they speak volumes to me of the sacrifice, love, care and patience Dan and Steph showered onto all of us. I can never fully express my gratitude for all my uncle's family did and gave.

But despite all the good food and care, I lost over 25 pounds in about six months, due to worry and stress. I was often self-focused. Where I had always been the queen of my castle, deciding what to cook, what to buy, what the kids were involved in, I had no choice but to relegate that to Steph, while I worked. I was now unsure of myself, my role. I lacked confidence and skills in the workplace, as it had been years since I worked outside of the home. I was very grateful to Steph for being there for my children, but I missed my "mom role." I missed my friends and my family and the loneliness continued to seep into my soul.

I had always thought of myself as a loving and forgiving person, but now I felt like a stranger in my own body, as anger often bubbled beneath my surface manifesting in ugly bursts of sharp responses, fits of crying and a sour countenance. Anger is much like a simmering pot. Let it simmer long enough, throw in some extra heat from bitterness, and, soon, it goes from simmer to boil. When it boils, it overflows. It doesn't recognize the blessings of the day but screams only for what it wants. The screams can often be silent, but eventually, they come out in the form of rage, rebellion or both. In the end, it is a desperate cry for help and a snare in which the enemy of our souls tries vehemently to keep us trapped. This is the place that I lived, inside of my heart and my head, for much of those months at Uncle Dan's.

You see, one can believe in Jesus Christ but still walk around with a wounded and bitter soul. This is why we must take the log out of our own eye before addressing the speck in another. (Mathew 7:4) God makes promises to us in His word, but some promises have conditions, and we must do our part before we can receive the promise.

I was good at justifying my bitterness. After all, I never wanted to sign the loan that resulted in us losing our home. Didn't I ask over and over again why this was necessary? Didn't I express concern? My perspective was that I was an innocent victim, and I had a right to rage because my life had been stolen. God allowed me to steep myself in self-pity for a while. It is not a place I ever want to go back to, but at that time, it was the only place I wanted to live. There is a personal gratification and self-righteous pride when we bask in self-pity. Beware! It has a serpent's sting!

Thankfully, His grace is not given because we deserve it. Thankfully, the price of forgiveness has been paid by the sacrifice of Jesus Christ on the cross. And, thankfully, God loves us enough, despite ourselves, that He eventually says, "OK, enough.

Trust me, God knows how to get our attention!

Chapter 10
Spring and Summer

"The grass withers, the flower fades, but the word of our God will stand forever."
(Isaiah 40:8)

My job, as an accounts payable clerk at the shoe store, went well. Ironically, I gained fresh office skills. I chuckle, now, to myself to think that as I write this book on a computer, back then, I did not even know how to turn on a computer. For reasons unknown, except due to the favor of God, my boss took a liking to me and gave me more responsibility.

I helped him with a photo shoot to put together his first retail brochure. I began to feel like maybe I had some undiscovered talents, and my self-worth increased slightly. But even so, that rage still simmered beneath my surface.

Rick continued to work at the uniform store. It wasn't until the day he resigned, months later, did I learn that this company was located in the roughest part of Southeast Washington, D.C. The front door was always locked, and clients had to ring a bell so that the door could be unlocked for them to enter. Rick could watch hookers and drug transactions go down on the corner, outside the building. He would be propositioned by prostitutes when walking to his car. But he never complained and continued to be faithful to do all he could to earn a paycheck.

Our friends, Pam and Tim, from Massachusetts, drove down to visit us. It was wonderful to see dear friends again. And when Rick's car died, Pam and Tim gave us their big, yellow LTD station wagon. Not good on gas, but it got our family around and got Rick to work!

We missed our many friends terribly. Carol and Lee sent us flowers with a Teddy Bear to hug me. Melanie called to check on me, often. My sisters endured hours of my sobs and complaints. My mom tried to encourage, and I know she prayed daily for us.

Eventually, we started attending a church in Maryland and met some new and amazing people. We were still pretty messed up, and I was often an emotional basket case, but our new friends took us in with love and care. Without some of these special friends, I am sure I am may not have emotionally survived. Nora and Larry, Patty and Mike, Lucy and Nick, Sheila and Dave, and Mannette and Neil were a few of our lifelines. Little did they know, each of them had a specific, divine assignment to help us heal our wounds and put our lives back together.

Through my friend, Lucy, we heard about a program in Montgomery County, Maryland, called Moderately Priced Dwelling Units

(MPDU). If a family financially qualified, the program offered a limited number of homes at below market cost. Several of our friends in our new church had applied for the program and encouraged us to do so.

Typically, the MPDU program worked on a lottery system, and once qualified, you could put your name in the ring for an available neighborhood development. Interestingly, a unique opportunity in a new neighborhood opened up, and it was not lottery, but first-come, first-served.

Rick and I filled out the paperwork that late spring. Our combined salaries put us at the top of allowable income; but still within the acceptable category for a family of five. Things were starting to look better, at last.

If I had to guess, I would say that Dan, Steph and the kids desperately needed a break from the five of us. They never complained, but they did plan a summer long trip out to the Grand Tetons National Park, in Wyoming, with several other stops along the way.

This left us alone, as a family, for the summer. In some ways, it was good.

It was nice to have the house to ourselves; especially the kitchen. It was a relief to have a place to cry without everyone hearing or seeing. The time was a needed weaning from the dependency of all the support Dan and Steph had given.

In other ways, it was very difficult. I had no child care, but I still had to work. I tried to find programs that I could afford, for the kids. I begged friends to babysit. I put the boys in a summer camp program near the shoe store. I would meet them for lunch. They hated being stuck there, and I hated leaving them there. Kim was in junior high and wanted to stay home alone. I felt "mom guilt" leaving her home, but I had no choice. I often cried on the way to work, after dropping off the boys.

Kim was forced to babysit when I had no other options. This was not the best situation for her or the boys. Sibling rivalry ensued. The challenges for all of us were many. I did the best I could. It was not the life I wanted for my children. I was not the mom I wanted to be.

Yet, there were blessings. I was able to work part-time, and we found a local pool we could join. I would get home by mid-afternoon and pile the kids in the car. We stopped for Slurpee's at the convenience store and then spent the afternoon at the pool.

I would, sometimes, pack a picnic dinner, and Rick would meet us there after work. I loved the water, and the pool seemed to help me wash away some of my rage and stress. It was the best part of that summer and I was so grateful for that place.

Dan and Steph eventually came back, and life resumed the normal routine; with all of us better because of the break.

By early fall, we found out we were accepted in the MPDU program for the neighborhood that was first-come, instead of lottery. We couldn't believe it. We were given our choice of lots. We picked the largest lot in the middle of Hourglass Way, Germantown. We knew, or hoped, that one day, we would be able to put in a swimming pool. All we had to do, now, was to secure financing for a mortgage, and once again, we would have a home of our own.

Sounds easy, right? Wrong! Having filed bankruptcy in Massachusetts created a huge problem for our credit. We went from lender to lender, only to be denied.

At this point, we had picked out the colors and cabinets and carpets for our new home. All was within finger-tip reach, and yet, all was so close to slipping through our hands. Could we possibly lose this second house? If ever we needed a miracle, it was now.

Just as our God is always faithful, He had already put the pieces in place for a miracle. We just didn't know it yet.

Chapter 11
Boss Angel

"Sojourn in this land, and I will be with you and will bless you, for to you and to your offspring I will give all these lands, and I will establish the oath that I swore to Abraham your father." (Genesis 26:3)

Rick and I did all we knew how to do to make moving into this home a reality. It was within the grasp of our fingertips, yet so far away. Bank after bank rejected our credit application for a mortgage. We were frustrated, confused, and upset that we had, seemingly, ruined our chances for a mortgage because of bankruptcy.

We prayed. We begged God. We walked around our almost finished home and claimed the house and property in the name of Jesus. We knew this house was meant for us, but the battle was not over. Then, one day, sitting in my office at the shoe store, with tears of frustration and discouragement silently rolling down my cheeks, I called one more time on the name of Jesus and told the spiritual adversarial forces to be bound. I loosed our home into our hands. I decreed and declared, according to God's Word, that this house was to be ours. Finally, something happened. Something broke in the unseen spirit realm; I knew it and I felt it.

God's Word tells us to decree a thing and it shall be established. (Job 22:28) He tells us to speak with faith as small as a mustard seed and speak to the mountain and it shall be moved. (Mathew 17:20) These are spiritual principles; upon which creation exists. And, they work!

A short time after–I honestly don't recall if it was days or hours–my boss, Ben, called me into his office. He, apparently, had heard some of the conversations I had on the phone with Rick, the banks, and the builder. Totally unsolicited and totally unexpected, he took me aside and made an amazing offer. Ben said he would finance the cost of our mortgage, at the current interest rate, and give us a year to get into our home and establish equity. We would, then, refinance and pay him back.

I stood in his office awash in unbelief. I was a part-time employee who had worked for him less than a year. Truly, this was beyond gracious. It was beyond favor. I could have never imagined, when I took this job, that God had strategically placed me there for such a time as this.

We humbly and gratefully accepted Ben's offer and were able to close on our loan and move into 11608 Hourglass Way, Germantown, Maryland, in October, 1987–one year and two months after moving into Uncle Dan's home.

As promised, approximately a year after moving into our home, we did refinance and pay Ben back. I will never forget the kindness this man offered. Yes, it was a business deal. But I know, in my heart, that God moved upon Ben's heart. To this day, I refer to him as my Jewish boss angel.

For God initially gave his promises to the nation of Israel and stated He would extend those blessings through Abraham and the Jewish nation. As a Gentile, who has come to a saving faith in Jesus Christ, I know that promise and those blessings were extended to me and my family.

This very promise was spoken over Rick and I back in 1985, while we were still living in Massachusetts and attending Faith Bible Chapel. A visiting prophet/apostle, by the name of Mark Chironna, was invited to minister to the church for an entire weekend. Several times during that weekend, Mark had Holy Spirit inspired prophetic words for various people. He called Rick and I forward from among the crowd and spoke some very specific and accurate words over us; individually, and as a couple. Part of what he stated was that, as a couple, we would receive "the blessings of Abraham."

I still have the entire prophecy on a cassette tape, and sometimes, I listen again to remind myself of the goodness and greatness of God to have singled us out and given us that word–a word whose manifestation we have experienced over and over again.

That particular weekend of ministry is etched in my memory, because the anointing and the presence of God was so strong that the room seemed to be under a cloud of glory that could be felt and even seen. It was unlike anything I had experienced, up to that time. It was transformative, as the manifested power and glory of God fell down upon us. It was an intersection of heaven and earth. I even remember the song that Mark Chironna sang; appropriately called "Standing on Holy Ground." I will never forget it. I know now, years later, that many of those words, spoken prophetically by Mark on that weekend, did, indeed, come to pass in the lives of others.

A few years ago, I had a call from Melanie who was still working as a tour guide for a large travel agency. She had an opportunity to be in Washington, DC, and I jumped at the chance to see her, as it had been a long while. As we sat in her hotel room, sipping coffee and catching up on so many things, it was as if we had never been apart a day. The weekend of Mark Chironna and prophecy made its way into our conversation.

Melanie shared how Rob had been able to get access to many of the recorded cassette tapes from back in 1986, long before digital, and transcribed several of the words spoken over individuals from that weekend. She shared how words spoken over her daughter, Tara, had come to pass, exactly as prophesied. We marveled at the amazing and gracious God we serve.

We hugged, with grateful tears and knitted hearts, knowing how each of our lives had been repaired and restored in different, but complete ways. Yes, the blessings of Abraham flowed to us and made all the difference--not only to Rick and me, Rob and Melanie, but also to our children; our legacy and our heritage.

I don't know what we would have done without my boss angel, Ben, offering us that loan. But because he did, we were able to start our lives over again and move our children into a new home.

In case there are some skeptics reading this and you haven't quite yet come to see that all of this was the hand of God, in His perfect timing, it is important to note the nuances of how things played out. Rick was offered a better position at Adams-Burch just weeks before we closed on our home. His then salary of $25K, combined with my salary, was the maximum our family could earn to qualify for the MPDU program. Every puzzle piece fell into place at the exact moment it was needed.

Rick has now worked at this same company for over 30 years, advancing into senior management. Adams-Burch and Rick's boss, Dan, have been the greatest blessings and source of provision for our family. Our gratefulness is beyond words. Our gracious, heavenly Father knew all the details of the big picture extended right into retirement. None of the details of our life escape His loving gaze.

Another point, worth noting, is this new home on Hourglass Way, a raised ranch, split foyer, was the same model home as the one we lost in Massachusetts; giving credence to God's promise in the book of Joel that He would compensate for the years that the locust had eaten and restore what we had lost if we trusted in Him. (Joel 2:25) But God does not just restore and replace, He does one better, each time, because He is a good God that loves to give good gifts to His children. This raised ranch was actually bigger; with an additional bedroom.

Making good on a promise we made to God, in thanks for giving us this home, we put that extra bedroom to good use over the many years we lived there. Several of our children's friends, our own family, and many others have shared in our home; some staying for weeks and other for years. I believe we have had over 11 individuals or families living with us, at various times. Our home was always a place of safety, respite, provision and healing to others; just as it was to us.

I have not been in contact with my boss angel, Ben, for many years. I pray this book makes its way into his hands so that he may know what a blessing and impact he was to our family. I pray that others who read this book realize that God uses ordinary people to touch other people. Miracles often are made up of one person reaching out to touch another in need. I believe God blesses us so that we may bless others and reflect His goodness upon the earth. Do not disregard the prompting of God to reach out to help someone. It just may change their life and their legacy!

Chapter 12
New Beginnings

"Behold, I am doing a new thing; now it springs forth, do you not perceive it? I will make a way in the wilderness and rivers in the desert." (Isaiah 43:19)

Unpacking at the new house was fun. Our belongings had been in storage for over a year, so it was like Christmas rediscovering our own things. I, especially, was delighted to have my personal touches surround me.

Kim's bedroom was on the lower level, in the back corner. It had a large window and a pink rug. Perfect for a young teen. Shaun's room was next to hers in the front corner. A blue rug and big closet gave him privacy and plenty of room. They shared a bathroom which was perfect. Brian's room was on the main level next to ours, as he was still young.

There was even a spare room, which we used as a den/playroom. The kitchen was tiny, but the combined dining-living room was expansive enough to accommodate all of our family and friends. Out of that tiny kitchen came many, many meals, over holidays and special occasions.

The backyard was large and eventually we were able to build a screened porch and an in ground swimming pool; something we could have only dreamed about, back then.

Several of our neighbors were Christian. Their children befriended our children. Of noteworthy mention were Sheila and Dave Leo, who, over the years, truly became surrogate parents to Brian. They watched him while I worked and took care of him when he was sick, until I could get home from the office. They took him on their family outings. Dave taught Brian to fish. They both showed him so much love. To this day, I am forever grateful. Brian holds a special place in his heart toward them.

Rick started his new job at Adams-Burch as operations manager in October 1987; the same month we moved into our home. Adams-Burch was a family-owned business, and the owners were amazing and kind people, who took us in as family. Neither we, nor they, could have possibly known how Rick's new job and his future part in this company would be strategic to our lives and the path God had planned for us.

It was truly God who lead Rick to that blind ad and put him in a place where the trauma of the past and the financial disasters of our previous mistakes could be healed and restored. After all the lost opportunities in Massachusetts, and all of the trials with Rick faithfully serving at UPS and every other job he held, Adams-Burch was to become the best opportunity of Rick's career, and, over the years, a vehicle of blessing to our family beyond our imagination; into Rick's retirement years!

I continued on at the shoe store for a few more years before taking a full-time corporate job. I was hired to work for a large, international corporation; to a position as a marketing and events manger. The job was well above my qualifications. I had minimal business experience and no college degree. But God's favor shone upon me, and I grew into more responsibility, developed skills, and uncovered talents I did not know I had. I created a successful and lucrative career that lasted almost 20 years.

Our children settled into school and youth groups. Finally, it felt like our lives were getting back on track. It should have all been great. Probably would have been great if not for unforgiveness, selfishness and rebellion. I was the culprit for all of them. I didn't like that my new life was so different from my old life. I now had to work to help pay the bills. I was no longer a full-time mom. I missed my friends and had very little time to make new ones. I was full of self-pity and regret; always living in the past.

I knew none of this was purposefully Rick's fault, but someone had to be the scapegoat and I was too immature and too angry to realize how I was hurting him, myself, and our family.

To be bluntly honest, in those early days, I was an emotional mess and not fun to be around. I think back to first meeting Nora, Sheila, and Lucy at church; they took me into their church care group. They prayed with me and for me. They listened to countless hours of complaining, with tears. They loved me, corrected me, and stayed with me through it all.

It wasn't like there was one thing. I just never allowed myself to accept what had happened. I felt like I was innocent in all of this, yet I had to pay the consequences of Rick decisions; which I never fully supported. I was stuck in the muck of the past.

There are snippets in my mind of my actions during that time. I remember our marriage had become so stressed that at night when we laid in bed, I did not want any part of my body to even rub up against his. I remember standing in the bedroom one day, complaining to God. I clearly said, "God, this is not fair, this is not what I signed up for. I am a victim." God clearly responded back, "It was not fair what Jesus went through for you. He was a true victim; yet, He willingly died for your sins." Those words, though not audibly spoken by God, were as clear and sharp as could be, in my spirit. It was a startling wake up call, and it required me to stop feeling sorry for myself and start getting my act together.

But that is not to say it was at all easy or that I changed overnight. Not even close. For several months, maybe even longer, the trauma of all that happened, my unwillingness to let go of my old storybook, fairytale life, became a dagger between me and Rick. It was truly my hard heart that was the problem.

God had to bring me to a place where I would fall so low that the only place back was up. I was destroying my marriage, and though Rick had hung in there, despite it all, one final blow was about to take us down.

I wish I could erase all of my stupid decisions, harsh words, unforgiving and resentful heart. I wish with all my heart that I did not have to write this chapter. But, if this chapter did not exist, I could not tell of the great mercy and restoration and healing that gives God, the glory. For that reason alone, to give God the glory due to Him for His miraculous healings and grace, do I allow this chapter to find its way into print?

Some of the reason it has taken me over 30 years to write this book is because I knew my children would read it. I struggled, in my heart, to take ownership of my grievous sin and to ruthlessly call black, *black*. My greatest shame and fear has been in uncovering my greatest failure. The courage it took to honestly write this story is my declaration that fear will no longer dictate, control or influence me. For God has not given me a spirt of fear, but of love. So, my story continues.

In my arrogance, pride, anger, and rebellion, I broke our marriage vows. If anyone would have told me that I was even capable of doing this, I would have never believed it was possible. I was a strong, Christian woman. I knew better. I did love Rick, but I had allowed my hard heart to cause a chasm between us. I let ego and pride trap me. When it all happened, I was so upset with myself that I confided in one of the ladies in our care group, asking for prayer. I knew God had forgiven me, but I needed to forgive myself. I thought they would pray and all would be well.

Well, all was not well. An unexpected bomb went off. The woman I shared my secret with gave me an ultimatum. She said if I did not tell Rick, she would. The reason was because, unless this secret was brought out into the light, there could never be true healing and forgiveness. I was furious. How dare she? But deep inside, I knew she was right. I struggled for days and finally agreed. I told Rick with fear, trepidation, and the deepest sorrow I had ever felt. Then, I sat back and watched, as the aftermath of that bomb exploded all over him. He was wounded deeply. The months that followed were the result of my reaping what I had sown.

I remember staying home from work, waiting for everyone to leave the house, and getting on my knees with the drapes in our bedroom still drawn. I cried-no wept and wept-until there were no more tears, and my body heaved until it fell in an exhausted pile of brokenness. I cried not only because of the stupid decisions I had made, I cried not only because I deeply hurt Rick, I cried not only because my marriage and family lay in the balance, but I wept out of deep conviction; much like David did in 2 Samuel 24:17, "I alone have sinned and done wrong. For it is against you and you alone, God that I have sinned."

Despite David falling from grace and sleeping with Bathsheba, after repenting and grieving at the consequences of his baby dying, he got up, washed his face and went on with life. And God, in His mercy, still saw David as a "man after God's own heart." These were profound lessons that cut deep into my heart and gave me hope.

With true repentance came forgiveness and grace. If this chapter did not exist, I would not have experienced the depth of grace that comes from receiving, not only God's complete forgiveness, but the forgiveness of myself. The words in the gospel of Luke chapter 7, verse 47, became a lifeline to me: "Therefore, I say to you, her sins, which are many, are forgiven, for she loves much. But she who has been forgiven little, loves little."

I knew I had been forgiven much and, therefore, I could now forgive and love much. God began to heal my angry heart and restore my feelings of love for Rick. I had never stopped loving him. I just allowed my wall of anger to keep that love from expressing itself. But just because we repent, there are still consequences that do not magically go away. Yes, I started coming around, but the hurt that I inflicted on Rick was now causing him to react. Frankly, he had every right do so. God was dealing with both of us in different ways.

Did you ever drop a delicate glass vase onto a hard surface, like cement? It doesn't just break into large pieces and chunks; it shatters into shards. It splinters into a million little pieces. That is what happens when a heart is broken. It takes a skillful hand to gather the tiny broken pieces, with sharp edges, and put them back together into a seamless life. Likewise, when a house is in full disarray, sometimes you have to tear it down to the very foundation in order to build again. That was exactly what was happening in each of our lives. But thankfully, God's skillful hand was at work behind the scenes and despite us.

I remember, with great detail and pain, a conversation we had on Mother's Day. It was a warm, even hot, May day, and we went to

Seneca Park to talk. We sat on the grass, on top of a hill overlooking the lake, in an uncomfortable silence. Rick looked at me and said, "Donna, I don't know anything anymore. I don't know if I believe in God. I don't know if I want to be married. I don't know if I want to be married to you." I supposed I deserved it, but now that I was starting to heal and feel love for him again, those words stung like a knife piercing my heart. I finally understood what he must have felt. What could I say?

The Holy Spirit said I was to pray and say nothing. I was to give Rick the time he needed to sort things out. I was to fight for my marriage in prayer. And so, for several months, I did, as Rick worked things out in his own way. I shut my mouth and prayed when he did not come from work until late. I shut my mouth and prayed when he played loud music, when he suddenly cared about what clothes he wore, and angrily peeled out of the driveway. I cried and prayed at the thought of us having gone through so much, to be so close to losing it all, when I finally knew I wanted my marriage to be saved. I trembled at the thought that Rick would feel justified to do to me what I did to him.

The best way I can describe that season is to say that it was like the Holy Spirit put a muzzle on my mouth. Even if I wanted to react, unpleasant words would not come out. But despite my late efforts, it got so bad, at one point that we actually talked about divorce and who would get which child. I summoned all of my prayer partners, especially Nora. They prayed for both of us and they loved Rick and me, despite ourselves. Larry, Dave, and Mike reached out to Rick, but never pushed him. They just let him know he had friends.

During that time, Rick had a vivid dream—or several dreams. In his recurring dreams, he was fighting three giants; the third was the largest and most dangerous of all. I believe the battle that Rick fought was lived out in his examining every facet of the foundations of his life; from faith and belief in God, to his love for me, and his desire for marriage and family. He fought, day by day, not only symbolically in his dreams, as the unseen demonic world fought for his soul and our lives, but in the decisions he made, daily. To this day, Rick will say, "Love is a decision we choose to make."

Little by little, my husband began to come back to me and our family. He began to smile again. When I told him I loved him, he said, "I know. I can feel it." Then, one day, I found a card on the kitchen table with my name on it. In this one, Rick wrote:

"Thank you for not giving up on me. Over the last couple of weeks, I have really felt your love for me, and I have felt my love for you grow again. I know my mind is still messed up in

some areas, but I guess these are things I have to deal with. The good news is, I spend a lot more time, lately, thinking about you, me, and the kids, instead of just me. Forever and a day, Rick."

And on another day, I found this card, where Rick simply writes, *"I want to keep making memories with you."*

I still have those cards tucked into my Bible.

Little by little, prayer by prayer, decision by decision, our marriage began to heal. For God's mercy is new every morning; over 30 years later, now and forever, I will keep those two cards in my Bible. They are a tangible reminder of God's goodness, mercy, forgiveness, breakthrough, and restoration. No one is immune from falling into sin. Thankfully, God's grace is able to restore us.

When the time was right, we renewed our marriage vows, and we did so, again, on our 40th anniversary; set in a beautiful vineyard, in Italy. Those two cards are a testament to the man that Rick is and always was. His forgiveness was complete and his love ever-faithful.

Those cards, handwritten, tear stained, with lessons too-hard learned, are a cornerstone in our family legacy. I often shudder to think of what I would have missed and how our lives would be so different had we both not been willing to forgive and allow God to break us, so that He could heal us.

I do wish I knew, then, what I now know about how to heal the wounds and traumas that life and sin inflict on our souls. Knowing how Jesus heals our souls is key to living a fully abundant life and fulfilling our God-given destiny.

I am so grateful for God's hand upon my life. But I am also aware that we have a part to play in our own healing. We can choose to be victims or victors.

Chapter 13
Memories and Memorials

"They are living memorials to declare that the Lord is upright and faithful to His promises."(Psalm 92:15)

This chapter brings us almost full circle to the title of this book, *Treasures in Darkness: More Precious than Silver; More Costly than Gold.*

The title comes from several of my life verses: Isaiah 45:3, "And I will give you the treasure of darkness and hidden riches of secret places, THAT you might KNOW it is I, the Lord, the God of Israel, who calls you by name" (emphasis added); Psalm 66:10, "For you have proved us and refined us as silver, refined, and purified;" and Job: 23:10, "For you know the way I take, and when you try me, I will come forth as refined gold, pure and luminous."

In order for gold and silver to become precious metals, they must go through fire so that the dross and impurities are removed. Otherwise, they will not shine. The summary of our story is our journey through the fire, as a result of the decisions we made. Beyond that, and more importantly, it is our story of God's faithfulness; with the end goal that we may know Him more and personally.

Throughout the scriptures, God tells His people to take time to build altars and memorials of remembrance along their path as a reminder of the great and mighty things He has done for them. Moses, Joshua, Jacob and others stopped and took stones from the places of God's intervention and built memorials in those specific locations and moments in time; where and when God met them. These altars were to serve as a reminder of great miracles to the people of that day and to future generations. Sometimes, the intervention was in the form of angelic help; to win a strategic battle against Israel's enemies. Sometimes, it was supernatural provision like water coming out the rock that Moses struck or manna in the dessert. Sometimes, it was supernatural phenomena displayed in the natural realm; like the parting of the Red Sea or the plagues of Egypt. But whatever the story or the circumstance, the people were to remember the might, power, protection, and goodness of their God.

The New Testament tells us that we are "living stones." (1Peter 2:5) Our story is known by the way we live our lives which is our testimony. We are told to share the wonderous deeds of our God so that future generations may know the unsurpassed greatness of their God and take hold of the spiritual legacy that is left to them. For we overcome by the blood of the Lamb and the word of our testimony! (Revelations 12:11)

We are also told to remember the good things God has done for us and forget not his many benefits. One of the practical ways I remember is with Christmas ornaments. One of my favorites is the porcelain, hand-painted star that depicts a dark winter scene. There is one bright star shining on the dark night's path, lighting the way, to signify God's light in our darkest moments.

It is in this context that I write this chapter on living memorial stones.

Our story continues from the 1990's, until today. My children are grown and successful. We are blessed with six beautiful grandchildren. We lived at 11608 Hourglass Way for over 30 years, until late 2018. We, then, moved to an amazing property, surrounded by mountains and beauty in western Loudon County, Virginia, as we look toward retirement. Every morning and every sunset, we marvel at how it could be that we have come so far!

But let me not forget from where we came and take a moment to erect some memorial stones to the many interventions from my God, through the years. The interventions vary from provision or protection to assurance that God is real and with us.

The following stories are in no particular order or sequence of time. They are just memories that I dare not forget and I must pass on, with duty and thanksgiving, as part of our legacy to my children, grandchildren, and great-grandchildren, yet to be born. Perhaps, they will remind you of your own personal God interventions. Let us travel together down memorial lane!

∞ Brian was six or seven years old. It was bedtime, and I sent him up to his room, saying I would be up in a few minutes to tuck him in. After finishing what I was doing, I went upstairs about five or ten minutes later. Brian sat wide-eyed in his bed; his eyes bigger than I had ever seen them. He told me, in great detail, of having just seen angels descending a staircase that went from outside right through the exterior wall of his bedroom. He witnessed a battle between angels and other entities taking place in his room. Then standing at the foot of his bed, Brian described a large, tall angel in great detail. The angel had a white gown and a gold sash. He was powerful, yet kind. His eyes looked directly at Brian and said, "You do not ever have to be afraid." Brian felt the angel was actually Jesus.

∞ While in Massachusetts, Kim had always attended small, Christian schools. When we could no longer afford this, after moving and bankruptcy, she was forced to go to the local, public high school. In her defense, it was a rough school, racially diverse, and she had not been prepared to deal with this. She would call me at lunch time, crying, because she had no friends and no one to go to lunch with. Kim hated school. It got so bad, that I didn't know what to do. Finally, I decided to approach the principal of a small, Christian High School, where a few of her church friends attended. I prayed and put on my boldest voice and told the principal, respectfully, but forcefully, that I could not afford the tuition, but my daughter needed to be there. He allowed her to attend through her high school years and there she met her best friend, Holly, who remains to today, the sister that Kim never had.

∞ In somewhat a similar situation, Shaun was supposed to attend that same rough high school, as that was our home district. However, by God's grace, Shaun was friends with the son of the superintendent of schools. We petitioned for Shaun to be allowed to attend Damascus High, a much-preferred school, located one town away. The superintendent made an exception and allowed Shaun to attend. Somehow, we worked out the logistics until he was a senior and able to get an inexpensive car. Today, Shaun lives in Damascus and his two boys will attend that same high school.

∞ We were away on a trip. Kim was about 18 and driving home. In front of her was a dump truck with rocks. After hitting a bump, a rock came loose and was hurling directly at her. As it approached, on track to crash through the windshield and hit her in the face. All of this taking only seconds, the rock suddenly changed trajectory. Though it did go through the window, shattering glass over Kim's head, the actual rock landed in the back seat, missing her. Angels on assignment?

∞ Rick was driving home from work. A young teen with no license "borrowed" the family car and was driving in the wrong direction, heading straight for him. She hit him head on, going about 40 miles per hour. The car sustained damage, but the air bags did not deploy and miraculously, neither Rick, nor his coworker, were injured.

∞ I got involved in a group at our church called "mercy ministries." I started going to a women's homeless shelter to serve and share Jesus. Having lost our own home, this was an issue close to my heart. At the shelter, I met another woman from our church, named Jean.

Jean worked in Human Resources for a large, international company. I gave her my résumé and thought nothing more of it. Unexpectedly, a few months later, I got a call for an interview and landed the job, for which I was not really qualified. That job launched a 20-year career that was a financial blessing to our family and showed me I could do so much more than I ever realized.

∞ One night, a colleague and friend, Ken, came into my office. Ken and his wife, Jan, lived in Texas, and his flight home, that night, got cancelled. I invited him to our home for dinner and to meet Rick. We had talked about how it was difficult for me to work full-time,
because I felt I was not there enough for the kids, but we had accumulated a lot of debt when Rick was out of work. We had a lovely dinner and a few days later, Ken contacted me and asked how much debt we owed. As best as I can recall, it was about 10K. Ken told me that he had discussed our situation with his wife, and they wanted to give us a loan, at no interest, to pay off the debt. This was an unsolicited intervention and blessing. We paid off the debt and paid Ken and Jan back within a short time.

∞ My uncle was dying. He was in Massachusetts. I was in Maryland. I was not particularly fond of him, due to things he had done, but the Lord had put him heavily on my heart. I prayed that I would have an opportunity to visit him and pray with him, as he did not know the Lord. I had already bought a ticket to go to Massachusetts to see my mother for her birthday. My grandmother had died a short while before, and they were moving her from Florida to Massachusetts on the very weekend I had already planned to be there. I prayed, again, that I would have an opportunity to visit with my uncle while there, as I knew it would be the only time. I specifically prayed that he would be in the hospital and I could see him alone, without my aunt.

Upon returning to mom's house from grandmother's memorial service, her phone rang, and my aunt told her my uncle was back in the hospital. I knew God was setting things up for me to go pray with him. The next day, my sister and I drove into Boston to see him. As we entered the floor where his hospital room was located, we ran into my cousins on their way out. My uncle was alone. He was unable to speak, because his voice box had been removed. I asked him if we could pray. He wrote "yes" on piece of paper. We led him to the Lord. He wrote that we would never know how grateful he was. He died a few days later. The scenario unfolded exactly as I had prayed, in exactly the time I needed before I had to fly back home.

∞ When we first moved to Maryland, there was an issue with the IRS because our accountant, in Massachusetts, had not paid back taxes when the business closed. Without warning, we received a letter stating the IRS was putting a lean on Rick's paycheck until about $18K in owed taxes were paid. A family member graciously came to our rescue.

∞ I've already told the story of how we were able to move into our first home in Maryland because of favor through the MPDU program and the generosity of my boss angel, Ben. But this memorial is worth mentioning, again, as it was a huge turning point in our lives, and this act of kindness moved us into our destiny. Our home became an extended blessing and a safe harbor for many who stayed with us through the years.

∞ More recently, an $80K loan that we took out so that we could right-side our upside-down mortgage, in order to refinance at a lower rate, was unbelievably and unexpectedly forgiven with the stroke of a pen. Yes, 80K owed yesterday, forgiven today. The details of that story are for another time, but as I write this, it occurs to me that God provided recompense; for it was the stroke of a pen that caused us to lose our home back in 1986.

These may not be magnanimous miracles in the eyes of some. But they made all the difference in our lives. They confirm that God cares, not only about the big things--like restoring our home and our marriage--but also the little things that we want and need to live an abundant life.

I share just a few of the many, many interventions and miracles; for which I am so humbly grateful. All are monuments of remembrance and thankfulness to a good and faithful God. They are memorials in our family legacy.

However, I would be remiss if I did not point out that God often uses people to extend His blessings. We have always had many wonderful and generous people that were placed in our lives. We do not forget them. To that end, Rick and I try, always, to remember that to whom much is given, much is required. We strive to bless others whenever we can. We acknowledge that all blessings and good gifts come from God, and He expects us to be generous and to steward well. Someday, we will account for our stewardship of His blessings; for we are living memorial stones, and we represent the hands and feet of God on earth. We are exhorted to reach out to each other in mercy, kindness, and His love. People will respond to our actions before our words.

We all can look around us and see a need that we can meet or a person that needs comfort, companionship, or an ear to listen. Yes, we are busy, but we are needed. The world is full of people who struggle and feel alone. Meeting practical needs is critical but the healing salve of mercy and friendship is priceless. Let us not forsake the part we have to play in someone else's destiny.

Chapter 14
Tale of Grace

"Now to Him Who is able to (carry out His purpose) and to do superabundantly more than all we can dare ask or think (infinitely beyond our greatest prayers, hopes or dreams) according to His power that is at work in us." (Ephesians 3:20)

I started out this story likening it to a fairytale. I was the princess and I married my prince charming. We moved from the fairytale to a nightmare. But God moved us from a nightmare to a tale of grace. "For by grace, we are saved, through faith, not of our own doing but it is a gift of God" (Ephesians 2:8).

The most wonderful, amazing thing about "grace" is that it is an ongoing process. It is not a one-time event. We don't have to worry that we used up all of our grace allotment for life. It is a gift that we do not deserve, but we are given grace over and over again. We experience its wonders daily.

It doesn't mean we never again have hard times or that we do not have to fight for victory. It does mean we have the privilege of praying and trusting God for ourselves, our children, our grandchildren, and generations beyond. I like to use the phrase "praying it forward." It is like skipping stones on the water of eternity.

The ripples of prayer extend beyond the visible horizon. And the effects of prayer and grace change history and destinies!

I would not want to, again, go through the trials and tests of the past. I can say, with sincerity, that I am grateful for the wisdom and protection of God through it all. He, alone, sees the full picture. I know that, without having gone through these trials, we would be different people. Our lives, and our children's lives, would have taken a different path. I also know the lessons we learned, the endurance we gained, and the faith we developed were not just for our story, but so that we can now encourage others.

I am grateful for my children, their spouses, my grandchildren, my friends and all the opportunities that have opened to us since we left Massachusetts. Trusting God to take our pain and turn it into gain is not easy; nor for the faint of heart. But He never fails us. His faithfulness is assured and His mercies new every morning–if we will just believe and let go. We don't know what tomorrow will bring. But we do know who holds tomorrow in His hand. I also know that our history does not have to determine our destiny. He has given us what we need to make changes. And He has given us free will to choose.

Treasures in Darkness

There are *treasures found in darkness* throughout this story. I don't want you to miss them. So, like a miner who goes deep and sorts through the dirt to find the nuggets of gold and silver, I offer you some things worth pondering. Once you ponder, consider what unpolished gems lay hidden in your own life. When you discover even one, then polish until it shines with faith.

Nuggets of Gold and Silver:

- We are all sinners, but God is always ready to forgive.
- We must repent and ask for forgiveness, which we receive through the shed blood of Jesus Christ; because of His sacrifice on the cross, on our behalf. Then we must receive fully the forgiveness for which Christ paid such a high price out of love for us.
- A personal relationship with Jesus Christ is foundational to forgiveness and healing.

- After receiving God's forgiveness, we must move forward.
- God always has been, He presently is, and He always will be. We live in the limited dimension of time. God transcends our knowledge of time.
- To everything, there is a season. Seasons do not last forever.
- Our trials may seem like they will last forever, but, to those that love and trust Him, God promises to work out all things for our good. Then we can stand back and watch the amazing things He will do.
- Delay is not always denial. There is an appointed time and season for all things. Sometimes, we are right where we need to be, even when it makes no sense.
- Don't ignore warning signs. Discernment is a tool given to us by the Holy Spirit.
- Don't get trapped in the "blame game." Forgive quickly; move forward.
- Prayer changes things, when we pray in accordance to God's will, through His Word.
- The same mercies and blessings in my story are also available to you. God has no favorites. He loves us all.

- We do reap what we sow. But grace can be greater than our consequences if we turn all over to God. He, alone can work out all the mess of our lives into good.
- Bitterness is a poison of the heart and the soul. It shows itself in ugliness and discontentment, inside and out, and can block our prayers and our blessings.
- Sometimes we are the answer and the miracle to someone else's prayer. Step out in faith to obey. God blesses us so that we might bless others.
- Sometimes the victory is in just getting through the day.
- God is so much bigger, greater, and more powerful than we are able to comprehend. He often does more than we can dare to dream or imagine.
- We do have a free will. We either work with God, in alignment with His Word, or we work toward our own agenda. Surrender and trust are vital in living in alignment with Him.
- Using our voice to speak and declare and decree God's Word and promises, as truth, is a powerful weapon. Words create. They produce life and

- blessing or curse and death. We choose.
- Sin has a ripple effect; hurting not only others, but ourselves, more than we know. It actually wounds our soul.
- The wounds in our souls can impact our life on every level, even being passed down through the generations and our bloodline. Those wounds can affect our health, finances, relationships, emotions, and our ability to mature in spiritual matters.
- God wants to heal our wounds, body, and soul. Jesus said he came that believers may have life in fullness and abundance. (John 10:10)
- Living in the past and holding on to regret is harmful. It keeps us stuck. Living in the past can prevent us from receiving all that God has for us, now and in the future.
- God uses people to touch lives. You just might be someone's miracle. Listen and obey, so that you do not waste the opportunities to touch lives and alter destinies.

I was recently listening to a teaching, which shed an interesting light on the story of the demoniac man (Mark 5:4-6). The story tells of this tortured man, bound in chains and shackles, living amongst the "tombs." Another meaning of "tomb" is a memorial to the memory of the past. Unlike the memorials God told his people to erect to remember the great things He did for them, this scenario shows that when we live constantly in our past, we are shackled and bound in chains. We live in torment of mistakes, regrets, and memories we refuse to let go. Our movements and our boundaries are limited by our chains. We need the power of God to set us free, so we can move on, and into the future and blessings He has for us.

Life can be very hard. Life can be unexpected and unfair. Life can hurt. Moving beyond the place where we have been deeply wounded may feel impossible, at times. We all need help, at times, to move forward. Staying stuck in our hurt and grief is akin to living in the cemetery among the tombs. God wants us to walk in life and light; in healing, freedom, and restoration.

I shudder to think of what life might have turned out to be had Rick and I not chosen to forgive and move past the pain and the trial. If we could have had a tiny, an ever so tiny, glimpse into what God had planned for us, we would not have hesitated--we would have run, full speed ahead, toward Him and His amazing plan of restoration. Even so, I realize that, for many, it may seem too late. Decisions were made that are now regretted. But what is impossible for us is possible for God. (Mark 10:27)

If I know anything about my God, it is that He is more than able to restore, replace, and renew. It may not always look like what you envision, but if you trust Him, give it all to Him-the pain, the unanswered questions, the betrayals, the lost hope-He promised that He *will* work all things to the good for those that love Him and have been called according to His purpose. (Romans 8:28) His plans are so much better than ours. His ways, so much higher than our ways. (Isaiah 55:9) He sees you. He knows you. He is waiting for you to surrender all to Him.

What we have gained is so much greater than anything we lost. Do you need to meet the God of grace, the God of healing, and the God of restoration? Ask Him into your life. What have you got to lose? What might you gain?

Chapter 15
Restoration

"He makes me to lie down in green pastures. He leads me beside still and restful waters. He refreshes and restores my Soul; He guides me in the paths of righteousness for His name sake."
(Psalm 23: 2-3)

If you have ever had a wound or a cut that became infected, you know that to even lightly touch it can be very painful. If that infection is not treated, it spreads. At minimum, it will make you sick; if ignored, it has the potential to kill you.

When I was a very young girl, I remember my mom and my aunt were crying in our kitchen. I learned that my uncle had cut himself on a piece of metal, at work, and did not pay it much mind. A red line began making its way up his arm, and when he finally went to the doctor, my uncle was rushed to the hospital. The infection was quickly traveling through his body, heading straight for his heart. He was in danger of dying from a small, but uncared for puncture, that became an infected wound. The hospital gave him heavy, intravenous antibiotics, in just the nick of time, and he did survive.

I have an aunt that I loved dearly. Audrey was my cousin Joe's mom. She was instrumental in leading me to the Lord. She was like a second mom to me, in many ways. She began to feel ill, but my uncle was out of town and she wanted to wait for him to return to take her to the doctor. She waited too long to go to the hospital. Her condition became septic, and within a week, she died. It was heart breaking.

I was at the gym and the trainer had me working with ropes. I didn't have gloves on and got a rope burn. A few hours later, my finger began to swell. I put a topical antibiotic on it but the next day it was red, puffy, and very swollen. I waited a day or so, sure that the topical cream would kick in. It only got worse, until I went to an emergency, walk-in clinic. The infection was under my skin and my hand was so swollen, I could not make a fist; not to mention how painful it was. In order to get underneath, where the infection lived, the doctor had to dig under the top layer of skin, which had become callous to protect itself. The skin on the top was so hard that the doctor could not actually see where the origin of the wound was. He had to numb my hand and dig around in order to lance the blister and drain the infection. Not pretty. Not fun. Not really my fault–well maybe it was my fault, because I didn't put on gloves. But I didn't realize I needed to wear gloves, until it was too late. Unfortunately, ignorance does not eliminate the consequences. Likewise, the scriptures say, "My people are destroyed for lack of knowledge" (Hosea 4:6).

If we could see deep into the inner layers of ourselves, we would all see that we have wounds, many wounds. Some obvious, some deeply hidden in our inner most being. Often, we will develop a callous, protective outer layer, just as my hand did, because it is too painful to dig deep. But the festering, inside, does not stop because the outside has become hardened. Anger, offense, unforgiveness and bitterness are some of the ways infection festers inside of our souls. Our callousness can mask the origin of our infection. It may take painful probing and a skillful hand to reach the source. Fortunately, the Holy Spirit knows just how to take us to the place we need to be.

While writing this book, the emotions that overcame me, at times, showed clearly that, though it is over 30 years later, and even though all has been forgiven and life is truly very good, when I touched on a certain thought or recalled a poignant memory, it was still painful--even to the point of tears being evoked as I wrote. This is called "cellular memory." It means that thoughts, memories and emotions which are scientifically proven to be energy forms, take residence and are stored throughout your body, in your actual cells.

We don't have time to explore the facts of this conversation in this book, but it is a fascinating study to read about organ transplants and how the recipients of a transplanted organ often wake up with the memories, and even the desires and tastes, that were part of the life of the organ giver. I encourage you to explore this topic.

These traumas stored in our wounded souls must be released and healed so we can move into the fullness of all God has for us. God knows these things. He created us. He has not left me, nor you, to walk through life without the help we need to drain the infection and heal our wounds.

Jesus, Himself, was wounded. The difference is that He willing allowed those wounds to be inflicted on Him for us–so that we might receive healing (Isaiah 53:5).

His deep wounds left scars. As the Son of God, who was resurrected from the dead, I am sure He could have chosen to heal His own scars. One word from Jesus's mouth and those scars would have vanished.

Yet, the scars remain in His hands and feet, as a reminder of the great sacrifice Jesus made for you and for me.

Jesus told doubting Thomas to touch His scarred hands, as validation that it was truly

Jesus. But I believe there was another reason Jesus told Thomas to put his finger in the place of Jesus's scars. I believe it was to free Thomas from the doubt and allow Him to press on toward His destiny. The scars begin at the cross, but they move past the tomb and into the resurrection power of the risen Christ.

Our scars can be powerful reminders of what we have been through. We don't wear them as badges of honor. We bring them to the cross where the power of healing and forgiveness begins. Just as the callous in my hand had to be lanced and cleaned, so the infection could drain, we ask the blood of Jesus to cleanse us, and then we pray for the power of His resurrection to heal us. God promises to bind up our wounds, heal our brokenness, and give us beauty for ashes (Isaiah 61:3).

I believe almost every person has experienced soul wounds. These wounds can be the result of our own sin, the sins of another against us, or the traumas of life that we all face. Trauma can steal joy and even innocence that once may have brightly shone from younger eyes.

That is exactly what the enemy of our souls wants–to rob and destroy the good that God intended for us.

We must be proactive and fight for all God has promised us. We must align with His Word, not align with what we see through limited earthly sight. We walk by faith.

I do this by praying and declaring the word of God over my entire family every day. I claim the promises of restoration found throughout the scriptures. I circled the verse in Jeremiah 30:20 (NIV), which says, "Their children shall be as of old." I see, through eyes of faith, brokenness restored to the joy and peace of former days.

I continue to choose, daily, to see the manifested power of God in my life, and my children's lives, and in their children's lives. Healing is a process, and life is a walk of faith. I stand on the promises of God's word even when everything around me seems contrary. It is not always easy. I do not always do so happily, especially if my feelings contradict what I declare. But, in faith and in trust, I do it anyways. I rest my head at night knowing I have obeyed but the results are up to God.

God is a God, not only of salvation and eternity, but He is a very present help in time of trouble. (Psalm 46:1) Sometimes the battles we have fought for ourselves are training grounds for bigger battles to come. The word says we are to fight for our families in prayer, and then trust that God will arise on our behalf. (Nehemiah 4:14) We should never, never give up. God is on our side.

We have been given an incredible gift, once we choose to believe and receive Jesus as Lord and Savior. A simple and sincere prayer of trust and faith is all it takes. In return, we are given, not only forgiveness and eternal life, but God's word that says He desires for us to thrive not just survive. We had to do our part and cooperate with God, but He has never let us down – even when we did not understand why. Rick and I lived through the healing of many wounds throughout this story. We have scars that remind us of how far we've come. We have experienced supernatural healing and restoration from our brokenness. We have graciously been given beauty for our ashes; beauty in our marriage, with a love deeper now than ever. We experience beauty in our relationship with the Lord and His ongoing mercy and faithfulness. We have beauty in our children and the legacy of truly beautiful grandchildren, in whom we delight and find joy. (Isaiah 61:3)

We even have natural beauty that surrounds us every day. We look out of our windows and see breathtaking views of the mountains that flank us. We inhale the dewy freshness of the valley every morning. I hear His still, small voice in the gentle stream that meanders through our back yard. I am grateful for the freedom and joy of truth, as I watch butterflies play, eagles soar, and birds sing all around us. Each time I walk up to my front door, I pass the lilac bushes and pampas grass and roses bushes. I am reminded that God cares about the smallest details of our lives. He knows our hearts desires.

Truly, as the opening verse of this chapter states, He has restored our souls. Jesus is waiting to do the same for you. Will you let Him?

Chapter 16
All That I Ever Hope to Be

"What no eye has seen; What no ear has heard, what no human mind has conceived, the things God has prepared for those who love Him."(1Cor.2:9 NIV)

I do not want to live a life of religion. I want to live a life that is full of the resurrection power of Jesus Christ. I want my life and my family to experience this magnificent power, here and now–not just into eternity. I want my life to reflect all that God has promised in His word. I don't want to leave His promises and blessings on the table! I want to abide in His glory, live in victory, and be a vessel for that glory and light to shine into a dark world.

And, I want that for you. The word of God has the power to change your life. Its words are more than letters arranged on a page. They have self-sustaining power that reflects the heart of God. John 8:32 says, "You shall know the truth and the truth will set you free." It is my prayer that you find healing and refreshing for your soul, even as I have.

As for this part of my story, the pages of this book come to an end here. Our lives continue to be an adventure in Him. Rick and I celebrated our 46th wedding anniversary in May of 2019. We are older, have wrinkles and gray hair, but we are wiser. We know each other more deeply. We know our God more intimately. We know, not just in our heads, but in our hearts, because we have experienced that His goodness flows abundantly, and His faithfulness knows no end.

This does not mean that life is without ongoing challenges. Of course, we have difficult days and moments of frustration. However, it does mean we have faced fiery trails and our God has strengthened us as silver and gold. It does mean we have found treasures, earthly and eternal, in dark times and secret places. It does mean there is always hope, when you choose to trust God.

I want to leave you knowing that there is hope for you. I want to impart, to you, inspiration and courage to continue on. I pray your eyes be filled with faith to believe the best is yet to come.

I choose to close out by giving honor and glory that is due to God alone through this personal prayer.

"To My Lord"

There are no words that can thank you for you all are to me and all you have done for me.

Your kindness and faithfulness are so undeserved, yet, you shower me with your love daily.

Your presence is better, to me, than riches.

My heart explodes with my love and gratefulness for you.

I know that you have made me for a purpose and all that I hope to be is because of your goodness to me!

To You, alone I give praise and glory

Yes, Lord, to you alone all the glory that is due your name, I thank you that you have saved me, I thank you that you have forgiven me and washed me clean by your precious blood. I thank you that your plans for me are good plans and that I so look forward to the day that I see your face in eternity.

Now, Lord, I pray, you bless, protect and draw to you, each and every reader of this book.

May the words within these pages inspire them to know you and serve you because you are a good, good Father. To God Be the Glory for all He has done and all He will continue to do. Amen!

About The Author

Donna Gallagher loves to write about the goodness and power of her God. In addition to being an author and poet, she is a speaker to women groups and teacher of God's word. Donna founded Warrior Women of Faith Arise, an organization to help empower women to believe it is never too late to become all they were created to be. She would love to speak at your event.

Contact her at www.warrior-women.net Donna lives in Virginia with her husband. They have three adult children and six beautiful grandchildren. Donna's greatest passion is to leave a rich spiritual legacy to her family.

www.ingramcontent.com/pod-product-compliance
Lightning Source LLC
Chambersburg PA
CBHW072038110526
44592CB00012B/1474